I AM A
woman who

Recognising the Achievements of Women in Business

Foreword by
Jacqueline O'Donovan

By
Sandra Garlick

Published by:

Woman Who Limited

Number Three, Siskin Drive, Coventry, CV3 4FJ

www.womanwho.co.uk

First Edition
Published in Great Britain 2018

© Sandra Garlick 2018

Design by: Imaginate Creative Limited

Cover photography: © Simon Derviller

Copywriter: Rachel Garlick

Printed by: Reynolds Press Limited, Kenilworth

ISBN: 978-1-9996448-0-2

To Mum and Dad

*With my love and appreciation for
all that you do, without question.*

*Always there and continually
supportive with each and
every step I take.*

Contents

Acknowledgements:

This book stemmed from an idea brought to me by Sarah Young with the support of her MD, Joanne Derviller of Imaginate Creative Limited. Together they had a vision of how inspirational this book could be to others.

With special thanks to each and every one of the contributors who are all role models. Their honesty in writing their individual chapters has delivered content which inspires, educates and encourages women in business, wherever they are in their journey, to recognise their own achievements.

A huge thank you to Imaginate and Simon Derviller for supporting the photography and cover design throughout this project.

Thanks also to my niece, Rachel Garlick, for her attention to detail and efficiency copywriting and editing the content.

Thank you to June Picken, Director of Sales at Coombe Abbey for allowing us access to such a great venue for our photoshoot.

Thank you to the Woman Who... Judges who have each given their time so freely since January 2016: Paul Carvell, Ian O'Donnell MBE, Dr Sharon Redrobe OBE, Emma Heathcote-James, Debbie Davies, Linsey Luke and Angela Tellyn.

A special mention to Emma Heathcote-James who believed in Woman Who... from day one. She supported me with her time, listened to my ever evolving ideas and has championed Woman Who... throughout.

Finally, thank you to everyone who has been involved in Woman Who... since January 2016 including the Sponsors, Partners, the Federation of Small Businesses (FSB), Speakers and every woman who has attended an event or been involved in the annual Awards. It is a pleasure to watch you grow.

Sandra Garlick

A MESSAGE FROM

Sarah Young

I was introduced to Sandra Garlick and the Woman Who... Achieves Network through my MD, Joanne Derviller.

Joanne was nominated and won two awards at the Woman Who... Achieves Awards in in 2017. I was at the Awards, they were amazing. At this particular awards event we heard three inspiring keynote talks from fabulous women in business who talked about the highs and lows of their business journey. They shared their personal challenges too, yet they continued to be strong, committed and successful throughout their career, whether running their own business or working in a position within a business.

I found all these stories very inspiring and couldn't stop thinking about them. I found the more stories I heard at Woman Who... events throughout the year, the more I believed that other people should get the chance to read them too.

This motivated me to suggest we should create a book containing all these insightful and inspirational stories. I was thrilled when it was agreed. The idea was born, to showcase brilliant women role models and their inspiring stories that will motivate and encourage future generations to come.

I hope you enjoy reading these stories and feel as inspired as I do.

Jacqueline O'Donovan

MANAGING DIRECTOR
O'DONOVAN WASTE DISPOSAL

Encouraging women to flourish in business is a subject close to my heart and I am extremely honoured to have been asked to write the Foreword for 'I am a Woman Who.'

Whilst each of the stories are unique they share one common denominator – women who are truly inspirational and set a great example of how successful we can be irrespective of the challenges we may face along the way.

I know at first hand both the highs and lows of running a business. At the age of just 19 I found myself taking the reins of the family waste recycling firm following the sudden death of my father two years before. It was a harrowing time both personally and professionally.

I was working in an industry which was totally male dominated and although I had the support of my siblings, it was me in the front line.

The early years were tough. Given the fact I was so young

// Winner of the 2016 Businesswoman of the Year

I found I was simply not taken seriously by the banks and financiers – none of us were – however what this did instil was a steely determination to succeed and create a business which delivered exceptional levels of customer service on a par with what I would personally expect to receive.

It is this which has been my mantra throughout together with simple gut instinct.

From an early age I realised it was important to listen and learn from those around me and then forge my own way.

I am also passionate about providing my staff with the best tools for them to do their job, not just in terms of equipment, but also training so they can develop and build their own skill sets.

I am proud of what has been achieved over the years and can take comfort in the fact that I can go to sleep each night in the knowledge that we consistently deliver the highest levels of service possible and have simply done a good job.

I invite you to read these stories and my message to you would be don't be afraid to follow your instinct.

Sandra Garlick

FOUNDER AND DIRECTOR
WOMAN WHO...

"

REMEMBER, YOU CAN BE ANYTHING YOU
WANT TO BE. SOMETIMES YOU JUST NEED TO
STOP AND TAKE LOOK AT WHAT YOU HAVE
ACHIEVED SO FAR. LIFE IS NOT A REHEARSAL,
SO DON'T BE AFRAID TO TAKE EVERY
OPPORTUNITY THAT COMES YOUR WAY. YOU
MAY NOT GET ANOTHER CHANCE.

SANDRA GARLICK
WOMAN WHO...

I have met and been inspired by every woman in business in this book. I have watched their business journeys, their highs and their lows. Many of them have become friends and to me they are role models. I hope they inspire you with their honesty, passion, and determination to succeed, as they have inspired me.

Each of them is a real woman in business, not to be placed on a pedestal, but someone who will happily share their experiences with you.

If someone had told me when I was ten years old that I would be publishing a book, sharing stories from inspirational women in business role models I would have said, 'of course!'. If asked the same question as a teenager, I would have said, 'no way, I couldn't do that'. So where did that early confidence go?

Somewhere along my journey my confidence disappeared and the doubts in my ability took over; 'can I do that?', 'No, I can't', 'I'm not good enough'.

Sometimes, we just need role models. This book features some of my role models and those who act as role models to others.

My journey is no different to anyone else's. However, sometimes you just need someone to inspire you or show you the way, to help you recognise that you can achieve. Occasionally, you just need to stop, reflect, and look at what you have achieved to enable you to see where you are going, where your passion lies, and to help you set some goals for the future.

In January 2016, I fell and broke my ankle badly... and Woman

Who... was born. So, let's stop and rewind...

Here is my business story, the ethos behind Woman Who... and why I have brought these amazing and inspirational women in business role models together.

The Early Years

One thing I will always remember from my early childhood is that whenever I tripped and fell, my mother always said, 'pick yourself up, brush yourself down and you will be okay'. I have never forgotten it and didn't realise how much her words would become my mantra in later years. She also told me that I could be anything I wanted to be. Something I now realise is true.

1 in 100

Although shy in my early years, school changed all that. I was extremely confident and always the first to put my hand up to volunteer to ring the school bell, speak in assembly, or to help the teachers during break or lunch time.

I knew right then that I wanted to be a Doctor or a Lawyer. I could be anything I wanted to be.

Aged ten years old, my determined streak was already starting to show. I wanted so much to pass my 11 plus and go to a Girls Grammar School. Only the top 100 girls in the City were awarded a place and I desperately wanted to be one of them. I worked so hard to prepare for that exam and I remember the morning the envelope arrived with the result that I'd passed. I was elated. I'd set myself a goal and I achieved it.

Off we went to purchase my school uniform, which amongst other things included a navy pinafore, a beret, and the ugliest furry pants I have ever seen. The most exciting thing was choosing the shoes.

I soon realised that we looked like 100 clones, all dressed in identical outfits with similar looking black shoes. I no longer felt like an individual. My confidence drained, and I believed that I had to clone myself to become one of them. I hated my school years; I couldn't wait to leave. I switched off.

There were two thoughts about careers during this time, I could either work hard and go to University or become a good wife. No-one in my immediate family had gone to University, so I opted for the homely subjects such as Art, French, Cookery and Needlework. After all, I was being trained to be a good wife! I could cook a meal, speak French and do cross stitch! What more did I need?

Those early dreams of being a Doctor or a Lawyer were forgotten, I wasn't good enough or clever enough, despite my reports always saying I could do more if I didn't talk so much!

As my O Levels approached, I started to rebel. I no longer wanted to be labelled. I no longer wanted to conform, to be a clone. I found boys, discos, and fun. I wanted to earn money so I could buy clothes, and more importantly, shoes!

My first job

I'm a big believer in making the most of every opportunity that comes my way. Through the years, I've realised that I also create opportunities.

The evening before I was due to start Secretarial College, aged 16, my Dad said that he had seen an advertisement at work for Secretarial Trainees. The next day I applied, got an interview, and the very next day I started work at BL Cars (now Land Rover) in Solihull.

My confidence returned in that job interview. I really wanted that job. I could be anyone I wanted to be, and when asked if I could type, I said, 'of course.' Well, I had seen a typewriter and how hard could it be? When our typing teacher looked over my shoulder to see how I was getting on, I convinced her that I couldn't type if she was watching. A few weeks later we had our first typing exam. I passed with Distinction. My determined streak had returned.

The World of Work

During that year in Secretarial Training School we were seconded into different departments to cover for secretaries and PAs who were on annual leave or off sick. I loved the variety, the office structure, and especially working in the PR and HR departments. I knew that I could achieve more.

I saw an advertisement at the Midland Bank (now HSBC) for a typist. After all, I could type really well now, so I applied and got the job. After a few weeks, I knew that this wasn't the long-term job for me. I wanted to change direction and train to be a cashier. I went to see my boss. He wasn't very keen, however I managed to convince him that I would study hard at college during day release and focus on being a cashier. Begrudgingly, he approved the transfer. I was going to be cashier. I could be anything I wanted to be.

I did pass the banking exams and I did become a cashier... for a whole week, and then it all changed. I met a boy and got engaged.

Women in the bank didn't progress if there was a male coming through the ranks and I was told as I was soon to be married, I would be transferred to another smaller branch where I may get the chance to be a cashier. It didn't happen, so using my mother's mantra, I picked myself up, brushed myself down, and looked for another job.

Relying on my secretarial training, I managed to secure a role in Estate Agency as a PA. This was really fortunate as by this time I was married and we were selling our first house. A perk of the job was that staff paid no fees. Perfect.

An addition to the family

Quite unexpectedly, I found myself pregnant. It wasn't really in the plan as I was told I may never have children, but I was overjoyed. I was quite poorly in the early stages and decided to give up work and be a housewife. After all, that's what my mother had done.

I soon became bored.

Shortly before I gave birth, I applied for a part time role at Mothercare. I had heard that staff got 20% discount on goods. Ten days after giving birth, I started my new role at Mothercare and was given my 20% discount book. I also got a Sunday job back in Estate Agency in Stratford upon Avon as a Sales Negotiator. I loved it. However, I always knew I was capable of so much more.

In the years that followed, I realised that I was really good at selling myself and my skill set was growing. I became aware that my skills were transferable to other sectors, securing sales roles over the coming years in Estate Agency, Retail, Construction, and Communications. However, I always hit a barrier and couldn't progress. I needed qualifications.

Change happens when you least expect it

Shortly after my 30th birthday I walked out of my marriage with two small boys, in tow, aged four and seven, two bean bags, and a couple of suitcases. I now needed the support of my parents, who gave it willingly.

I will always remember the day I went to sign on for Income Support. I had nothing. I stood in the queue and said to myself, 'This is the last time I am coming here. I need to make a change and get a profession to give my boys the opportunity to be who they want to be.'

Somehow, I realised that despite being 30 I wasn't too old to completely change career. I walked across the road to the Job Centre and asked about training to be a Teacher. It was perfect... I would get all the school holidays with my boys, and how hard could it be? Fortunately, I made the wise decision to volunteer at the local school to get some teaching experience. I made a crucial discovery... I didn't like working with children!

I thought back to my early school years and decided right then that I wanted to train to become a Solicitor. I knew it would take eight years to qualify as I needed qualifications that were good enough to apply for University. I applied to two local Universities and was offered a place at both the following year.

Eight years is a long time, and although I had never heard of Goal Setting, this is what I did. I broke everything down into small chunks. Each year consisted of four quarters: autumn term, winter term, spring term, and summer, each consisting of 90 days. That's how I got through it.

1 in 3,500

I chose the University of Warwick as it was, at the time, in the top six Universities in the country for studying Law. It was also just one and a half miles from home. It was meant to be.

University was tough, especially studying and bringing up two young boys on my own, but again my parents came to the rescue and I was also fortunate enough to get a Sponsorship with Dibb Lupton Broomhead (now DLA Piper), one of the largest International law firms. The interview process was hard but I knew I had to get that Sponsorship. Failure was not an option for me, my boys and their future. I succeeded and was one of 50 applicants that year out of a total of 3,500 who secured sponsorship and a training contract with Dibb Lupton.

What next?

I qualified as a Solicitor. I had made it. I sat there and thought, what's next? All that work and I didn't feel any different. What was I supposed to do now? What was the next goal? I felt a little deflated. I was now 39... I couldn't change career again. I decided there and then that I wanted to become a Partner of a law firm. I had a new goal.

Sadly, it was going to take a very long time to achieve that goal where I was and I was spending huge periods of time working away from home. I moved to another firm, and subsequently to a firm nearer home.

I remember going to the Partners (six male, one female) with an idea about holding a women in business event. I had been researching and planning it for a couple of years. We would invite clients, contacts, and referrers to a morning with an inspirational speaker. We would provide light refreshments. I costed it out with a budget of £30 and mapped out a proposed guest list. I was told it would never catch on.

I subsequently handed in my notice and 90 days later, I was sat in my spare room with a laptop, a phone, a printer, and was the proud owner of a brand-new law firm. I was now a self-employed business owner.

Sometimes fate takes a hand

I worked hard in that law firm and grew it to be a niche Legal

500 Employment Law practice, one of the largest in the region. We were the 'go to' firm for employment law advice. I learnt so much about business. I'd never even heard about cash flow, forecasts, PAYE, and strategy for growth. It was a steep learning curve, but I loved it. In fact, I loved growing the business more than actually practising law, so I grew the team and spent most of my time working on strategy and business growth.

I started to network with other women in business. We all learnt about business together. They became my support network. My confidence in business grew and I started to secure voluntary Board positions as a Non-exec.

However, things change. The law changed in April 2015, and as a result our turnover plummeted overnight. I had to make some quick decisions. We had just moved into new premises I took out a loan and used the bank overdraft to keep the business going for the next three months. I had lease payments and salaries to pay. It was my responsibility.

However, after much soul searching, I decided that the only way to survive was to merge the firm. I needed to secure the future employment of my team. 90 days after initial discussions commenced we merged. I managed to save all the jobs, but to my own detriment. I didn't want to be an employee, and I no longer wanted to practice law, so I agreed to work during the transition. I used all the money I generated to keep up with the loan and premises payments. It was one of the toughest years I have ever had. I was exhausted working in the merged business and trying to set up a new business to generate extra income.

By January 2016, things were extremely tough. I was exhausted. I had no money, no income, and no direction. I had ceased working with the merged practice and was trying to generate an income to keep up with all the payments for a business I no longer owned.

Sometimes, when you least expect it, fate takes a hand and makes you stop and reflect.

On 16th January 2016 it snowed in Coventry. The only day it snowed that year. I slipped on a wet floor and fell. Embarrassed, hurt, and willing myself to stand up so I could brush myself down and get on with it... I couldn't. An operation, pins, steel plates, and six months on crutches wasn't in the plan.

I lost everything. I almost lost who I was as a person. I lost my focus. The Landlord pursued me and repossessed the premises, I ended a very one-sided relationship and distanced myself from a number of people who I thought were friends, but soon faded into oblivion when I no longer served their purpose.

I looked around for that support network. I found those women in business who knew exactly how I was feeling. They were there for me and helped me to get back on my feet. The mantra and determination kicked in and despite being on crutches, I brushed myself down and got on with it. I started getting consultancy work. I realised that I needed to stop, reflect, and make space in my life for change to happen. It was all about having the time to focus on who I really wanted to be.

A new chapter

I focused on being a Business Coach and Mentor. After all, it was on my goals list in 2009. In fact, I leant toward mentoring as I had such a unique skill set; marketing, sales, my legal and regulatory expertise, my business knowledge, and my innovative ideas for business growth. What's more, people wanted to pay me for that knowledge to help them grow their business.

I looked back at everything I had achieved over the years. Each project, new business, each and every idea I had written down broken down into 90-day chunks. It was a formula that worked. I now help my clients use that formula for their business growth.

Simultaneously, my son wanted some Event Management experience. Every time I have an idea for a business, I write it down, brainstorm it, cost it out, and then leave it to revisit in the future. I also buy any associated domain names, just in case. I went back to that women in business idea from ten years earlier.

Some said I wouldn't be able to achieve it and doubted that it would be a success. I ignored them and, spurred on by my support network, my determined streak won the day. On 15th

April 2016, just 90 Days after breaking my ankle, I hosted the first Woman Who... Achieves Awards (on crutches) with my son at the prestigious Coombe Abbey in Coventry. It was a one-off, or so I thought...

I realised that women in business sometimes needed to be reminded that they have achieved great things, whatever point they are at in their business journey, but often didn't have the confidence to recognise those achievements.

The Federation of Small Businesses released a report in April 2016 called *'Women in Enterprise: The Untapped Potential.'* I was invited to submit my CV to sit on the newly created FSB National Women in Enterprise Taskforce. I was successful and as well as a visit to Number 10 to speak about barriers experienced by women in business, it was also suggested that I set up a Network in my own region. It was important to me that there were no barriers, no membership or criteria, and that the Network was open to women in business (and men too) at any age and at whatever stage they were in their career or business. The aim was simple... to inspire women in business to recognise their achievements and to celebrate them. The Woman Who... Achieves Network was born. It now operates nationally and in partnership with the FSB in many regions.

I call Woman Who... my accidental business. It wouldn't have happened if I hadn't broken my ankle which in turn made me stop, reflect and think about my achievements. I needed to find my passion and to focus on what I needed to change to allow that to happen.

Woman Who... is not my main business, it's a community that sits alongside my business. I now focus on Business Mentoring, hold a number of Non-Exec positions and speak throughout the UK. In fact, I have even started delivering Speaker Masterclasses.

I am a Woman Who... inspires and creates role models of the future. I love to see the women who enter the Awards grow. They listen to the business stories of other women who inspire and act as role models. I see these women grow in confidence and their business support network grows too. For some of them it's a complete transformation. They enter the Awards one year and may not be selected as a Finalist but through the support of the Network and the women in business they meet, they are encouraged to enter again and even end up winning awards in subsequent years and become role models to others.

If you would like to feature as a role model in a future edition of this book then come along to a Woman Who... Achieves Network and begin your inspirational journey.

Sandra's top tip:

"Always remember that there is someone somewhere who has been in exactly the same position as you. Build a strong support network around you. Spend time with women in business who have similar values and inspire you, learn from them as they will have learned from their role models."

Sandra's favourite quote:

"Give a girl the right shoes and she can conquer the world."

Marilyn Monroe

www.sandragarlick.com www.womanwho.co.uk
www.speakermasterclass.co.uk

TWITTER NAME:
@SandraGarlick @WomanWhoAwards

Helen Routledge

CEO
TOTEM LEARNING

"

YOU WILL NEVER KNOW WHAT YOU ARE
CAPABLE OF UNTIL YOU TRY. YOU CAN GROW IN
UNIMAGINABLE WAYS. BEING AN ENTREPRENEUR
IS AN EXCITING JOURNEY, ONE WHERE YOU VERY
RARELY KNOW WHERE YOU ARE GOING TO END
UP! NEVER BE AFRAID OF CHANGE. EMBRACE
MISTAKES AS OPPORTUNITIES TO LEARN AND
MOST OF ALL ENJOY THE RIDE!

HELEN ROUTLEDGE
TOTEM LEARNING

Like many people in the Learning and Development (L&D) industry, I'm driven by a desire to help people fulfil their potential and I hope that by creating games that learners want to play repeatedly, our end users will rediscover that natural love of learning.

As a game designer, I believe in the power of stories. My motto in life is to live a story worth telling. So, let me tell you a story. A story about conquering demons, overcoming difficulties, and pushing boundaries.

When you think about the business journey, you often think about when you first founded your business, or the moment of inspiration which gave you the 'AHA' moment and confidence to take that first step. But my journey starts before I even knew what business was.

As a child, I was the most timid, shy, and compliant person you could imagine. I was brought up in quite a strict atmosphere, less academic than my older brother, and I felt little pressure to succeed. I didn't really try that hard and I told myself I wasn't any good at school, or work, or socialising. I had very poor self-esteem and absolutely zero confidence.

Until one day, Mrs Grant, my GCSE maths teacher told me I would fail and not get anywhere in life. Her words echo in my mind to this day, "You will not pass!". Almost like Gandalf on The Bridge of Khazad-dûm fighting the Balrog in Lord of the Rings. At that moment, something changed inside me. It was almost as if a switch was flicked and the light came on. This was my first 'AHA!' moment. Life was not just something that would simply happen, I would have to make things happen. And so I did. Although I was a teenager, it really formed the person I was to become and the business I was to help found. Fast forward a few years and I didn't fail, It was almost like I needed the challenge. I needed the cliff edge.

Around the same time as I got my behind in gear I discovered the mysteries of the human brain. I remember watching an Open University programme about how the brain worked and I was fascinated. I wanted to understand why people made the decisions and behaved the way they did. Psychology became a passionate hobby and I would read everything I could on the subject. When I wasn't reading I would be playing games at home with my brother and my friends. I loved the problem solving, the fact I had to work hard to complete each level, and most of all I loved the social aspect of sitting around the screen with people I cared about working towards a shared goal.

Unfortunately, I didn't quite pull my finger out enough to get the A-Level grades I needed to get into my University of choice, but, whether it was fate, or subconscious planning, I found myself at a university which was the hub of the games industry in the UK: The University of Abertay, Dundee. Lemmings and Grand Theft Auto were born in the city and I found myself immersed in games culture. I was there to study psychology and behavioural sciences and the more I learnt, the more I could see the connection between psychology and games. Game design is all about getting players to behave in certain ways, to follow certain paths willingly and to keep playing. Simply put: game mechanics tap into the way our brains work.

I soon knew I wanted to do something with games, and so I agonised over how I could combine my two passions. I met a couple of chaps from the games course who had spun out a business around games for training, and they needed a psychologist to evaluate their new game to help break into the training market and begin to shape a brand-new industry. How could I refuse that?!

My first foray into business was wonderful! TPLD was one of only three companies in the UK, founded in the same year, who were creating serious games. It was genuinely ground breaking and so exciting. I regularly travelled to the US to present at the growing number of conferences and typically as one of the few female speakers. As the shy wallflower, this was a huge challenge to me. I kept returning to my maths teacher and my 'AHA' moment; that life is what I make it. The pride, excitement and challenge, as I'm sure we all feel as entrepreneurs, pushed me forward and we made TPLD one of the global leaders in the sector.

After a while, evaluating other people's designs began to lose its appeal. I pushed to move into product design. Moving a function can be a challenge, I had to prove that I could do it, was capable, and would benefit the company. The original founder of TPLD was the game designer and he was understandably protective of his ideas. I made my case, grounded in facts and he finally agreed. I became the Product Manager for our educational product with a small team of developers. I had the responsibility of planning the future direction of that product, coming up with designs and directing the developers. I loved it. I worked directly with schools, the local and national authorities, and it was wonderful to see kids playing the game and having their own 'AHA' moments.

Eduteams became the most successful product that TPLD had produced and I'd like to share a little story about one group of girls I worked with while managing this product: four girls were going through the game and playing a module which was all about the future and where they saw themselves. They were all talking about the number of babies they would have and how much they would get in benefits. Now this was Dundee in 2005, the teenage single mum capital of Europe at the time, and so this was actually a reality for many young girls. I sat with these girls and talked this through with them, they had worked out the monthly costs, what cash they needed and what they would get per child. They had actually produced a great financial plan, just not for the world's next great business. They didn't even see the connection between their plans and great life skills until we picked it apart and they realised what they were capable of.

I truly feel privileged to have worked with so many kids on hopefully helping them realise their own potential.

TPLD attracted a CEO from a large UK organisation. He was brought in to grow the business and the revenues, however the entrepreneurial spirit of the company changed and I believe we lost our focus and USP. The opportunities started to reduce and I found myself frustrated. I decided to leave. This was a hard decision as I felt I was leaving a family, I had been with TPLD since just after its beginning and I was very attached, but it was time to spread my wings. I am a big believer in self-made luck, tell the universe what you want and it will listen. I started to tell people in my network that I was looking for opportunities and very soon something came up. PIXELearning had just moved into the newly launched Serious Games Institute in Coventry and needed an Instructional Designer. I jumped at the chance.

I discovered a strength for design and managing the development pipeline. I eventually ran the entire development team and we became very successful, disrupting the UK and US training and development industry with some of the largest organisations worldwide such as KPMG, 53 Bank, HP, and Comcast. The games we were producing made a real impact. The ROI (Return on Investment) of one of our projects demonstrated a $13.4m return in the first year alone from a $700,000 experiential audit training game.

PIXELearning was acquired by a large AIM listed eLearning company that had big plans to develop a consortium of learning and development companies – to provide a one stop shop if you will. At first this seemed like a great opportunity, but it soon emerged that HQ had very different views to our team. A new production lead was brought in to manage the team, so in effect I was given a demotion. Relationships soured and tensions grew. Unfortunately, due to a tough market, spiralling costs, and an overambitious strategy, the head office had no choice but to liquidate the entire group. The whole team was made redundant.

Typically, being made redundant is a bad thing, however, for me and the other members of PIXELearning it was one of the best things that happened to us. In all honestly we could see it coming. We tried our best to keep the company going, but in our own time we worked on plan B. So, in preparation we started putting plans together to start up our own company. On 31st October we were made redundant and on 1st November we started our new roles in Totem Learning. Our excellent relationship with clients helped migrate them to the new venture and we built a group of shareholders from the L&D community, who had knowledge and connections and believed in us and the business.

This time we had the opportunity to really plan. Previously, as is often the case in a nascent industry, growth is very organic and reactive. This time, we had a solid plan with the steps outlined for the next 5 years.

The relief was palpable. It was a new start, we were our own bosses. This meant we could build the products we believed the market needed and wanted. We started to produce more award-winning products around Leadership, Project Management, and Welding with proven ROI and increased retention rates.

Despite the growing market opportunities and award-winning products, it has become clear to me as I have progressed through my career that there is still the need to demystify technology for our clients; both in terms of the production process and what is possible with games hardware and software to realise what they can achieve in their businesses. Something I have always wanted to achieve was to write and publish a book. I've mentioned the term, 'the universe is listening', and since my early days in the industry with TPLD I had an outline written. I never did anything with it of course, apart from stare at it every now and again and dream. But with the new start of Totem and it being all about creating a sense of community, shared knowledge, and history, I made my dream known. I started telling people about my ideas, they told others and before I knew it I met someone who was a business book writer, had published many successful books, and was well connected with the world of publishing. My dream became a reality, 'Why Games Are Good for Business', was published in 2016 by Palgrave McMillan and became a practical toolkit for those who want to learn more about serious games and how to apply them in the workplace.

However, just after I secured the publishing deal I found

out I was pregnant. And so I was in a bit of a dilemma, do I risk postponing the opportunity for a year or do I challenge myself to get it done? There was the cliff edge again, my need for a challenge won.

I did what I could while I could, but the time came when I had to stop. It was a tough decision to take nine months out but it really made me appreciate the business, the people I worked with, and one of my key passions in life.

When I returned from maternity leave in 2015 I had to finish the book as the deadline was looming. It was also amazing to see how much had changed in the business in nine months. There were many new processes and faces, and I had to gain their trust as a leader. That was probably one of the hardest things I have ever had to do. It was quite a challenge, as at the time I was fighting Post-Natal Depression and Anxiety and I suffered terribly from imposter syndrome. I struggled to match the person I had become to the person I used to be. I paid for personal coaching, I tried to remember what I used to do, who I used to be. I tried to force things back to the way they were. But time moves on and people change. It took me a long time to realise that I should not chase the old me and instead embrace the new me.

I've never spoken out about this before formally (yet another challenge), but the universe is listening. I truly believe the way to feel better is to talk; by verbalising and facing the negativity it somehow loses its power. It won't beat me and I sincerely hope it won't beat anyone else. It's always hard to admit you are struggling and in the tech industry especially, being male dominated, there's extra pressure on women to perform and prove that we know our stuff. But if we don't talk about it, it becomes a pressure cooker and we all know what happens if we don't release the pressure.

Just when I felt I was getting a measure of stability in my life, in late 2016 my mother passed away from a very aggressive form of cancer and then three months later whilst dealing with her loss, our MD, friend, and one of our founders, Richard Smith, passed away suddenly and unexpectedly in early 2017. This was a massive shock to everyone at Totem, our clients, and supporters. Richard was not only our MD but also our one and only salesperson, making connections and driving the business forward. Richard was the heart and soul of Totem. From a purely commercial point of view losing this function can often be fatal to a small company, but also losing the MD could have been catastrophic. I had to step up into Richard's position to lead the team. At the time, we had three major projects running at difference stages, our bank account was frozen and we couldn't make any payments to any suppliers or staff. Because of the chaos that ensued we were threatened with court action three times in six months. Our investors were on the verge of pulling out and we had to face the real consideration of reducing the team or closing our doors altogether. I won't sugar coat it, it was the hardest time of my life, dealing with the loss of my mother, a dear friend and colleague, and managing the mounting business challenges, I did question many times if it was all worth it.

One of the best decisions I made was to seek help. Of course in times like this the offers of help always flood in, but finding the right help was paramount. I reached out to Spencer Holmes, who was in fact Richards's brother-in-law and one of our existing investors. Initially on an ad-hoc basis he helped with some of the day to day activities, the many conversations we had to have, chasing invoices, and adding a great deal of motivation and energy, all while he was dealing with this awful situation himself.

Once the shock had subsided and some tough decisions made we were forced to pause and re-evaluate the entire company. We rewrote the strategy, forged new partnerships, and expanded our geographical reach. It was almost as if we became a start up again.

The whole team pulled together and achieved a tremendous amount in incredibly difficult circumstances. I'm pleased to say Spencer has joined Totem as Chief Commercial Officer and together we made it through. We have had our most successful year yet, even winning internationally recognised industry awards. Everyone at Totem Learning has shown not only incredible resilience, but also unbelievable commitment.

The last year has taught me that life is short and can be hard, but I am determined to make it worthwhile, to live the story worth telling. To badly paraphrase Shakespeare, life is a game, and all the world are players so it is our responsibility to play the best damn game we can.

Helen's top tip:

"Life is short and fragile so follow your passion. Find something your truly enjoy, a reason for getting out of bed in the morning and grab it with both hands and never let go."

Helen's favourite quote:

"I hope that in this year to come, you make mistakes. Because if you are making mistakes, then you are making new things, trying new things, learning, living, pushing yourself, changing yourself, changing your world. You're doing things you've never done before, and more importantly, you're doing something."

Neil Gaiman

Website: www.totemlearning.com
Twitter: @helenroutledge

Emma Heathcote-James

FOUNDER/CEO
LITTLE SOAP COMPANY & LITTLE SOAP SCHOOL

"

ALWAYS SAY YES EVEN IF YOU DON'T KNOW
HOW YOU WILL DO IT. YOU CAN WORK THE
LOGISTICS OUT BEHIND CLOSED DOORS LATER.
'YES' IS A WORD THAT CREATES OPPORTUNITIES,
THAT ENABLES THE MAGIC TO HAPPEN.

EMMA HEATHCOTE-JAMES
LITTLE SOAP COMPANY
& LITTLE SOAP SCHOOL

My accidental journey starts by wanting to find a creative hobby to get me off my laptop and to start doing my own thing. My background was PhD research in the anthropology of religion which took me straight into broadcast and television research. A few years after moving to the Cotswolds I was desperate to put down roots, so I changed track and set up my own PR agency, concentrating on the creative industries in the South West. I was surrounded by creativity and loved every minute yet there was no room - let alone time - for me to be creative.

Then somehow, through a bizarre series of events culminating from the realisation you couldn't buy proper soap in the supermarkets, I started hand-making soap on the Aga. I was ready to start selling – farm shops first, then in sub-zero degrees at local farmers markets, craft shows and school fetes, then upscaling and producing literally hundreds of thousands of bars and liquid soaps in factories across England, becoming the first organic bar soap to line the shelves nationally of the UK's top end supermarkets...

Why Soap?

Growing up my beloved Granny always waxed lyrical about the virtues of proper soap. It was a staple at her and Grampa's house as it was indeed our own. When she died we found soaps stockpiled in paper bags in the back of her drawers and wardrobes – it was only as the stash started to dwindle that my mother and I started to try and find something akin. It soon became apparent you could only get proper, natural soap from specialist shops or even more impractically, Europe! You couldn't buy anything like it on the supermarket shelves in the UK and it enraged me. What's more, the 'soap' that was available in the supermarkets wasn't soap at all but synthetic copies full of chemicals. They made my skin tight. So, I started making my own.

The first attempts created a mess; crumbly or pliable custard like creations. It was only when I met a soap maker at a village fete my life was kicked onto a new trajectory as she told me the right oils to use – things I'd never even seen in their raw form let alone worked with – I was simply using store cupboard ingredients as the tatty library book I'd found told me to do so. Daft as it sounds – the internet in 2008 was far from what it is now, no buying online, no googling... there was Yahoo and Ask Jeeves and he had already proved he didn't know what made a good recipe!

I created the hobby business in 2008 and called it Naked Soap Company – we were in a recession and I was entering an industry I knew nothing about and in which all the experts were smugly quoting that bar soap was in decline. Suffice to say, I like a challenge.

Within a week I'd created a very simple website, a Facebook page, and quickly trademarked the logo but couldn't get the words marked as they were deemed descriptive. I designed and printed a bespoke box and labels for the soap and collated all my safety assessments, stability and challenge documentation, and insurance certificates, and within weeks had it lining the local farm shops and boutiques. But I wanted more. This soap was better than anything I had ever tried. It belonged in Waitrose. Through a series of calls I quickly found the right person, I emailed them, left a voicemail and even hand wrote a letter sending samples. Nothing.

Thinking locally, Warner's Budgens shops have a huge emphasis on local produce, yet you can still do a weekly shop in them. So, undeterred, I organised a meeting with their buyer. Sitting in his office, I splayed the various boxes in front of him, talking non-stop about how it was a no-brainer as it was made so locally, how there were no organic or handmade offerings on his shelves, how I'd love him to take it on and help me get the brand established, and well, you'd have thought I had created a Cotswold branch of Port Sunlight and had done him the biggest favour the way I went on...

Finally getting a word in, Steve, obviously bemused, asked a few questions about delivery cases, pallets and barcodes. Bewildered, I simply ignored the first two questions and asked could they not just put price stickers on the boxes as all the farm shops were doing? Steve leant over the desk, I don't think he actually called me 'sweetheart' but I felt the tone – he said he very much liked the product but to come back in a year or so when I was a bit bigger, had some feedback, and had barcoded products, then he'd review them.

My pride hit the floor – this was my first actual no. We laugh about it now, and I do credit Steve and his non-existent red rag I felt he was waving for helping me grow so quickly...

It was midafternoon and I arrived home in a blind fury. I asked Jeeves 'how do you get barcodes' and got on the phone – GS1. Now one of the biggest lessons I have learnt from the Little Soap Company is learning to ask for help. Or, on a more personal level – that asking for help doesn't mean failure.

My tack had become 'I'm sorry, I'm totally new to this so please speak to me like I'm an idiot'. It worked wonders, every time. I was on a mission.

I collected the sheet of barcodes at 9.30am next morning, took out my kitchen scissors and cut the sheet, cross checking the numbers, sticking the barcodes onto their respective products – then hopped in the car for the ten minute trip to Warner's Budgens.

Steve's door had a window in it – I hopped excitedly outside it, pointing to the gleaming black and white labels adorning the boxes... He smiled. And that was how we got into our first small chain.

It's been a terrific relationship and they've helped me in so many ways including sorting out my initial pricing structure.

In hindsight it was a rose-tinted introduction to the slightly bigger boys; they ordered by phone; I delivered in old wine boxes (we managed to bypass the casing and pallet conversation) usually the same day and was I always paid by the end of that month; I delivered to the store nearest me and they popped it on the next lorry to deliver to which ever one it was going to. It was perfect and so easy in terms of being a one-woman band. A gentle introduction!

Getting established: Ask, hold hands and sell, sell, sell...

Now with barcodes and three months trading under my belt, I tried Waitrose again with my new prices – presuming that explained their silence. But still I was ignored. So, I simply drove to Bracknell and door-stopped them, waiting in the foyer, befriending the receptionist who by 11.30am realised I was there for the duration so winked and pointed out the right buyer as she walked past me at lunch – I didn't realise this wasn't the done thing. I grabbed her on her way back. She explained the reason she hadn't replied was I was a 'kitchen table' business and had no scalability. No, I said, 'I don't need that – I just want you to put me in Cheltenham branch as that's where all my friends go.'

'I can't put you in one', she replied, 'I will trial you in eight as a local producer.' I became best friends with her assistant, the admin team, their IT team, anyone who would help me get through the tranche of forms and paperwork.

I launched. I learnt the term 'loss leader' first hand as I drove boxes of 12 bars to stores ranging from Birmingham, to Malvern and Cirencester, to Kenilworth. But, I was in Waitrose, just too mortified to admit to anyone I was self-funding the accolade!

Trademark

Fast forward 18 months - I was still working full time delivering, doing farmers markets, and producing soap in my spare time. The week before Christmas, a large American conglomerate obtained a license to use the word 'Naked' in class 3, and sent me a Cease and Desist. My patent attorneys worked on the case for six months without any payment, waiving the fees at the end when we all agreed it would be better for me to stop fighting and just change the name – and Little Soap Company was born. I didn't want to give up; it had legs and I wanted to make it work.

To recoup my costs, I set up Little Soap School. I worked my contracted hours in the evenings and ran Little Soap School by day.

Going it alone and filling the loneliness

Accidently, Little Soap School took off. I was doing three to four a week and thus working before and after making, packing, selling... Things went from being an idyllic hobby on the side to working 80+ hour weeks to fit everything in.

There was a physical cap on what I could produce too; it could only ever be a hobby. For it to really work, it needed to be volume, which of course is one of the main principles of selling – but to make in volume – by myself (to take on staff would affect the margins even more) was impossible as there weren't enough hours in the day.

Seek and ye shall find. Knock and the door will be opened unto you...

It was then I was asked to talk at a Women in Rural Enterprise conference. I almost said no as there weren't enough hours in the day, but I did it. Unbeknownst to me a Tesco Local buyer was in the audience. Afterwards, she arranged to come for an initial meeting at my house. Days later she came with someone from marketing and I gave them a tour of the workshop (basically the garage at the back of the house) and we went next door to the old National Trust pub for lunch – it was all very jolly. They left – it didn't really feel like a meeting with a huge supermarket – I liked them, it was as simple as that.

Tesco wanted to help us make affordable, make natural skincare a reality. Two thirds of the population shop at Tesco - 18 million people a week to be exact. I dithered for weeks.

It was at a dinner party when a friend's husband who works for a large food multiple, leant over and said, 'you were mad to walk away from that contract...no one offers contracts for products that don't exist – they must have really believed in you.'

His words echoed around my head, I had let them down – more so, I had let myself down. I called them the next morning. Full of questions, full of uncertainty – I needed to fulfil 25000 units of a soap bar, organic at my stipulation. There wasn't a delivery date – it was up to me to create it and make it happen.

All advice I read told me if you want to create a business you have to give it your all, so I wound up the remaining contracts I had and cut the apron ties to earning easy monthly money. It had to work now. There was no choice.

Setting up a business is lonely. I cannot emphasize this enough. No colleagues. The phone initially doesn't ring. Ridiculously long hours, no holidays, living mostly on savings as anything you earnt went straight back in, putting every waking hour into your baby. As I was incapable of any sort of work life balance I became a recluse –all I could speak about was soap and what I was doing, any other conversation felt superfluous.

I had a contract for a product that didn't actually exist but a contract I needed to take to a factory to make it happen. That contract was the biggest gift I have ever been given. It was this contract that enabled Little to go Large…

Going large with integrity (but with pain!)

In 2012 we rolled out into 45 Tesco stores and numerous local Cotswold outlets with the new cheaper range which was more accessible than the original handmade bars. Tesco was just the start of the new fork in the road for Little Soap Company. They gave me a spring board to make a noise and to offer up a real choice of soap on the shelves.

Time to roll out…

The pain of being able to deliver four products to Tesco meant through the blood, sweat, and tears I now had systems in place, a proven track record in delivery, relations, costs, and logistics and, as everything was working, it was time to roll this out properly.

I called Waitrose and sent in the four bars I'd launched. Immediately they asked if they could go national first with them. Of course!

The big game of supermarket chess: not liking being a pawn

In 2013 I launched two lines of the organic range with

Waitrose nationally, exclusively for two months then followed suit with Boots... The first English made organic bar to go nationally into stores...

I approached the other supermarkets, I didn't know how to pitch aside seeing Dragons Den. In meetings I cheerily spoke about Granny, showing the handmade bar and now the manufactured bar. Silence. The first buyer I saw had a poker face and remained tight lipped – 'I have numerous companies pitching organic soap every week, it's not a customer need here, why should I take it?'

I'd not expected that, so launched into an unrehearsed why... I came out with an agreement that she would allocate shelf space and we would launch in the next window.

Tesco saw Waitrose had gone national, did their sums and agreed we'd go national there too.

With more supermarket accounts secured, the decision to apply and be invited in March 2014 to go on the Goldman Sachs 10kSB course was the singularly most impactful decision I've made for the business. I went in thinking I had such a clever business model working from home, not needing to employ anyone, and having so much cash in the bank, but I came out the other side a changed woman. It made me face up to my limitations, realise 18-hour days that I had normalised weren't sustainable, and that I needed to take on staff and a premises to operate from fast if I was to become investable for the future. And stay healthy.

Moving off the kitchen table...

Taking on a team (eventually) transformed my life and the business. But as any start-up will tell you – the pain of trying to defrag your brain and download information was nothing short of painful, time consuming, and so easy to moan that it would be quicker doing it yourself. On top, choosing the right people.

The best team has come from selecting like-minded people who share my values and interests in an organic, healthy life style; they have all been taught about soap from the bottom up, in the workshop; and then about business, or rather the way I want MY business to run: with integrity, ethics, focus, and passion. One of the messages that's at the heart is customer service and transparency.

More products – more problems?!

Within 12 months the team created and launched an entire new exclusive range into Waitrose. Then the first major issue hit. As the shelves were being filled it became apparent that a previous trial formulation for the bubble bath had accidently been made by the factory – one oil was omitted, others were listed that weren't in it, and frankly it wasn't the product it said it was.

Transparency has always been key, as has honesty. I decided to withdraw the product that day. There was an admin fee, costs per store to take it off the shelves, and a cost to destroy the stock. Tens of thousands of pounds.

We needed the replacement product asap, with no time move to another factory. Waitrose had empty shelves - so I agreed, through gritted teeth, to split the costs with the factory and give them a second chance. We got new product to stores within a week and I could sleep at night, not worried about being discovered as misleading our customers. I then moved factories!

2016 was good. We'd also started to make organic soap for several top skincare companies under their own brand. I was fast achieving my business goals and on a personal level my partner and I had recently moved into our dream barn conversion together. For the first time I was taking proper holidays and able to work some days from home. We were set to turn the £1m figure, we were living in the £1m barn, and set a date to get married - all goals I had set to achieve before my 40th birthday. Things were comfortable – yes, I still worked too much, but genuinely I wanted for nothing.

The next test....

Then the rug was unexpectedly pulled. My fiancée was arrested on several counts and my relationship ended overnight. My carefully constructed world was suddenly in freefall.

Unsurprisingly I developed pneumonia but I had to press on at work. One morning a month later my mobile woke me early. It was our main manufacturer calling to say as of 9am that morning, they were going into Administration. Out of the blue my business world was suddenly spiralling too.

It was critical for the business that the factory fulfilled the scheduled orders for the supermarkets. We had no stock, non-deliveries, empty shelves, fines, and the threat of being delisted. There wasn't time to get our packaging to another factory as lead times are around 6-12 weeks. I drove four hours to Bury that afternoon to speak to the Administrators who wouldn't take my calls. They agreed to keep the factory open and to make those orders and to create three months stock to give me time (bearing in mind this took in the Christmas period) to organise other factories.

However, the Administrators wouldn't do warehousing. I had no choice to agree to a vast percentage being added to each unit cost and pay a six figure lump sum by the end of the month as the gates shut. I said yes to everything, fathoming I'd work out how later.

I spoke to my bank and secured the money immediately, however, over the next week it became clear they – nor anyone – wouldn't be able to get me the money in full so fast. It'd take nearer 4-6 weeks.

The only other option was to put my money where my mouth was and sell the dream barn. Two phone calls later I had two buyers. One agreed a £100k deposit to be paid to me immediately to secure the sale. In return, I agreed to move out within the month.

It fast became evident that the whole business model had to change. We sourced a depot and logistics to fulfil orders ourselves. Despite the warehouse costs, this gave us more control and flexibility, not to mention proper stock in hand for the first time.

Running a business needs quick thought, problem solving, and flexibility. Time ran out and the Administrators hurriedly sent unpackaged bars of soap to the depot. Totally useless to us! Fortunately, I had recently been introduced to a local women's prison who were thrilled to take on the project and they boxed/labelled thousands of bars for us.

I paid the Administrators in full, and in October 2016 moved into rented accommodation on a farm. Tiny converted stables –a safe place I could start to get well and get the business back on track...

During this time, I was heralded Coventry Telegraph Business Awards Entrepreneur of the Year and also made the finals of the Lloyds National Business Awards. Two events I had to literally crawl out of bed to attend, wearing heels, a now very baggy dress, and smile as if all was normal. Suffice to say, as predicted just four months later, the business paid me back in full.

The (tired!) phoenix...

My team went above and beyond during this stressful time. One small family run factory grew their turnover with our substantial runs to the extent they've increased their staff and bought machinery, enabling us to grow together.

We came out the other side. Yes, our Gross Profit took a massive hit but we countered it as we were rolled into more stores in two of our supermarkets.

It was good to see the back of 2016, and 2017 felt like a period of rebuilding myself and the business. I was in an incredible new relationship, and had an adorable 11-year old step-son in my life who was fast opening my eyes to what life really is about. That year, I took my foot off the gas and gave myself permission to learn to live a more hygge way of being. I hit 40 and the year was about concentrating on my new family and friends, getting well, and learning to laugh again. I outsourced things to experts which turned out to be key and critical to the business moving forwards. The new internal and external team was amazing. By conducting them, it became the best year yet, personally and professionally.

We still launched two new sensitive skin lines for Waitrose, as well as creating a series of Gift Sets and a Hamper for Christmas. We got all our products approved by The Vegan Society, and developed and secured a new Naturals Range which launched nationally this March... The growth continued, as our key buyer put it, 'at a phenomenal rate.'

What a difference a decade makes!

So now in 2018 – ten years since I started this 'hobby business' – with a key team and eight outsourced experts, we are focusing on our own retail website and Amazon. We're launching a new unisex blend and new lines of organic shower gel, lotion, and shampoo and conditioner which will complete the range and enable us to create a suite of minis for hotels which will launch early summer. As for my home life – we are getting married this summer.

The business is in a far stronger position now than it has ever been. We have backup procedures and factories for our backups, and we've revisited everything and refocused. Although I wouldn't wish any of the difficulties we've experienced on anyone, we are stronger having got through the other side – professionally and personally.

The company is growing at a phenomenal rate, forecasting a hugely exciting scalable business with a steady track record that's set to grow year on year. It's only since we hit the £1m turnover – despite still being incredibly small – that I finally felt in a place where I could hold my head high and proudly admit I've turned a kitchen table hobby into a proper business. A hobby which was the first company in its first year of trading to be taken on by Waitrose, and the first organic bar to nationally hit supermarket shelves. A business with the passionate aim running through its core to give consumers a choice of what they rub into their skin... the accidental entrepreneur.

"

THE MORE IT SCARES, YOU THE MORE VEHEMENTLY YOU SHOULD SHOUT 'YES'. 'PEOPLE DO BUSINESS WITH PEOPLE' IS ONE OF THE MOST PROFOUND LESSONS I THINK I EVER LEARNED. YOU CAN MAKE YOUR BUSINESS OR BREAK IT. SAY YES. SEIZE OPPORTUNITIES WITH BOTH HANDS. LISTEN. PUT YOURSELF OUT THERE. YOU NEVER KNOW WHO YOU MAY MEET OR BE PUT IN TOUCH WITH AND HOW THAT WILL CHANGE YOUR BUSINESS, AND IN TURN YOUR LIFE...."

Emma's top tip:

"People say don't start a business unless it involves doing something you absolutely love and are good at (unless you have an overriding passion to do something, then dedicate yourself to becoming that expert over the coming years as I did). Then, launch before you feel ready. I have seen so many start-ups procrastinate, and waiting until your product or service feels perfect means you're giving someone else the opportunity to be doing a better job of helping your customers solve their problems, and thus losing money. Launch quickly, find a small group of paying customers, then adapt to make your solution great for them over time. "

Emma's favourite quote:

"I strongly believe the business of a business is to improve the world."

Marc Benioff

www.littlesoapcompany.co.uk

TWITTER NAME:
@Emma_H_J   @Little_Soap_Co

Fleur Sexton

MANAGING DIRECTOR
PET-Xi TRAINING

"

DON'T BE SURPRISED WHEN THINGS
GO WRONG; IT IS PART OF THE JOURNEY.
BE RESILIENT. IF YOU FALL, GET UP
AND FIND A SOLUTION, RATHER THAN
WALLOW IN DESPAIR.

FLEUR SEXTON
PET-Xi TRAINING

I am co-founder and Managing Director of PET-Xi Training and 2017/2018 UK Business Woman of the Year. I believe in education and community to empower. I am married, a mum of three children, and have four dogs.

My business started 22 years ago. Previously, I was working as a teacher in North Paris, it was a difficult area and there was next to no opportunity. It was difficult to engage the students as they just weren't interested, I needed to get them into a different mindset and to believe that there were opportunities and possibilities. It's where I first developed techniques for barrier breaking.

Following this, I then went on to work at Exhall Grange where I worked with students who were blind. It is extremely difficult to teach children without sight to learn another language, I learned just how resilient young people are and how there is always a way. I wrote a course to help the students learn French because the curriculum at the time didn't meet their needs, and I didn't want their lack of sight to be a barrier to learning another language.

That is where it all started...

I had no business training or a business plan, no plans to start a business or make money. I simply wanted to create a product that was specifically for those children, and that is what we did, and what we continue to do – help people learn and develop through engagement and barrier-breaking.

I've always led with my strengths and although we've grown significantly over 22 years (we've scaled to 500 full-time and part-time staff), many of my key responsibilities have remained the same throughout. In addition to having overall responsibility for the financial and business success of the company, I am also responsible for directing the ongoing primary training activities. This growth has enabled me to explore and develop additional opportunities and responsibilities, such as our community involvement and has allowed me to focus more time, once again, on the part closest to my heart: working directly with learners and young people.

Since 1995, PET-Xi has helped over 100,000 young people across England and Wales achieve their potential and progress along their chosen pathways through its signature high-impact intensive training programmes. We now work with hundreds of businesses helping people upgrade their skills and move on with their careers, as well as working with people who are either trying to return to work, or to get into it for the first time due to facing significant barriers.

My responsibilities cover the work we do across England and Wales, from our main headquarters in Coventry, to our satellite offices in Sheffield and Hull which allow us to better focus on specific individual local projects . I have overall responsibility for all business functions, the training programmes (which ones we offer, how they are designed and written) which I find especially interesting, our trainers (how we deliver our programmes, how we train our trainers), and for ensuring that every single programme we deliver has our "Xi" (eXplosive Inspiration) methodology throughout. This methodology is the approach and style with which we engage learners, build their confidence, and help them take ownership of their learning and progress to achieve their potential. There are no 'off days' when you are entrusted with learners' time and it's my responsibility to ensure that every single programme delivers the best it can for every single learner, every single day. Without initially realising, I have been developing this methodology since the beginning of my career; from working as a teacher in Paris, at Exhall Grange, as a mainstream school teacher teaching Juniors through to A-Level looking for the most effective ways to engage learners, through the early days of the business' evolution devising and delivering 100% of our training programmes, right through to the present day, where on any one day up to 70 teams of four trainers can be running a wide range of courses across England and Wales, in schools and businesses of all sizes.

I am committed to finding and establishing additional routes to support young people, for example, I established the PET-Xi Foundation in 2014 to provide direct 'no red tape' support for anything that young people need to break down barriers and enable their progression.

I value the communities we live and work in and am dedicated to improving them, always with a special focus on breaking barriers and enriching the lives of young people within them. For example, our £50,000 sponsorship of Coventry's bid to be the UK City of Culture 2021 has (in true PET-Xi style) been full of activities by, with, and for young people. These include a roadshow to schools in Coventry and Warwickshire and a video produced by young people expressing how much they love Coventry. Also, alongside the Coventry Blaze Ice Hockey Team I have helped collect food for the homeless and distribute toys to children in need. Through my love of the theatre I am proud to sponsor the Birmingham Hippodrome and directly support their community work - for example - my staff and I volunteered to help with their first 'relaxed' productions, where the theatre environment is adapted so that people on the autistic spectrum or with communication disorders can best enjoy the theatre with their families.

I am optimistic, enthusiastic, and resilient. These skills help me to never give up on any learner and I am a true believer in second chances. No one is ever beyond help. This is a fundamental principle of our methodology in working with learners, and is reflected in how we train our staff. It also allows me to turn negatives into positives; six years ago a change in government policy effectively cancelled the vocational qualifications which represented two-thirds of our revenue. This needed a strong response in the face of such a change and our response became one of my biggest achievements to date. Despite having a two-week old baby, I designed and wrote new revision products for GCSE (then a completely new area) and we risked our house to provide the finance to launch them to prevent staff from losing their jobs. Our GCSE 'High-5' programmes launched to huge success. We had a 94% success rate in helping students move from a grade D to a grade C – great results, which improved the career and further education prospects of the young people we worked with.

I consider myself a good leader and am passionate about people. Being a leader is not just about leading people to drive business growth, it is primarily about service and about inspiring the people you work with to give their best. These skills are even more instrumental in shaping our approach to working with learners of all ages (an approach called 'relentlessly optimistic' by one educational journalist).

I am very proud that we still have the same inclusive family culture we had when we first started the business, even though we now have over 500 employees. I am deeply committed to maintaining PET-Xi's own family feel. I love the idea of family as, 'a group of imperfect people who refuse to give up on each other'.

Our staff are committed to the company and our values. Our latest employee satisfaction survey reported that staff feel 'highly valued' and produced an amazing overall score of 92% compared to the UK average of 68%. Getting to know our staff and their families on a personal level is also an important aspect. I also interview every potential member of staff to ensure they fit into our dynamic and energetic atmosphere. This is essential in the work we do to get the best results for the learners we work with, whether someone is working directly with learners at the front end or a member of back-office staff, and it is important for the well-being and progression of our staff and crucial for the long-term stability and growth of PET-Xi. This year I am working hard on growing the business further, developing the business training side and, in particular, an IT qualification for businesses and English and Maths for adults.

Becoming a successful business leader has not been easy and has required resilience and a genuine love for what I do. Since becoming Business Woman of the Year, I am frequently asked for my top business tips for aspiring entrepreneurs.

For me the key points are:

Build your network

Networking is about building long-term relationships and a good reputation over time. It's about meeting business leaders with whom you have synergy, getting to know people who you can assist, and who can potentially help you in return.

Look up your old contacts and give them a call. If you are setting up a new business a personal referral from a former colleague or client to a new customer can do a lot to help fast track your business.

There is also truth in the phrase 'it's lonely at the top' when tough business decisions that aren't appropriate to discuss with staff need to be made. Surround yourself with other business leaders who can provide you with the support and advice you require; a problem shared is a problem solved. Always be prepared to return the favour.

Empower yourself

Be resilient and be prepared to re-invent yourself. What worked today won't necessarily work tomorrow. Time moves on, trends, policies, and issues change, so make sure you have the solution to meeting the current challenges facing your clients.

Champion women in business

I love the saying 'Real queens fix each other's crowns.' We need to help each other up when we get knocked down and need to support and nurture each other and build alliances.

Extend the reach of your support of staff beyond the focus on the working day – for example, being family-friendly by accommodating the needs of working mums. One size does not fit all so reinvent the rules if need be. 20% of our staff are working mums and all of them have valuable skills to bring to the mix, so we make a concerted effort to try and make their life easier. For example, by providing free childcare daily. This has done much to strengthen camaraderie and loyalty.

Invest in training

Most employees have some weaknesses in terms of their workplace skills. A well thought out training programme will enable them, and you, to develop and strengthen those skills, helping employees to feel more valued, confident, and happy.

Remember the 'return to work' mums - those who have had a career break to look after their children. Everyone has something to give but some just need a little help to sharpen up their IT skills. Train them and you can create close allies - and remember happy employees make happy clients.

Inspiring and helping people achieve their full potential is at the heart of everything I do. From young people and their communities, to women and those considering starting a business for themselves. I will continue to share all elements of my story in the hope that any part resonates and helps them.

Fleur's top tip:

"Make the rules to fit the people, rather than find people to fit the rules. If you make rules to fit your staff and ensure you have a good work life balance, it will be significantly easier to create a happy and productive workforce. Stressed staff working long hours typically don't deliver long term. "

Fleur's favourite quote:

"Real queens fix each other's crowns."

Celebrate other women, help each other to be strong and build resilience and pick each other up when we are down.

www.pet-xi.co.uk

TWITTER NAME:
@FleurSexton

Gurdip Chatha

MANAGING DIRECTOR
ESQUÉ BEAUTY

"

SUCCESS IS NEVER A STEADY GROWTH, THERE
WILL BE UPS AND DOWNS, SOMETIMES YOU'LL
FEEL YOU ARE TAKING STEPS BACKWARDS BUT
NEVER GIVE UP... YOU'LL GET THERE IN THE END.

GURDIP CHATHA
ESQUÉ BEAUTY

It's always lovely when you are asked to share your story. I guess I've always just 'done what I've done', however, when I hear other people tell their stories it always amazes me. I hope I do that for you in some way.

Winning awards is something we do regularly for the business, it helps clients have conviction that they are going to a reputable establishment for their beauty needs. When I was nominated for an award personally I was blown away! As many business owners, you strive to do the best you can for your staff, it's just 'what we do'. To be recognised for that is very humbling. I won the title of Woman Who... 'Outstanding & Inspirational' Leader in 2017.

So, this is my business story...

It started when I was ten. My parents bought their first newspaper shop and myself, my three brothers and sister all had to do our bit. My father established business language from the beginning - we never received pocket money; instead we were paid a wage. On top of working our shifts we would help with trips to the Cash & Carry, pricing stock, and restocking. If a paper round needed doing if someone had called in sick, it wasn't unheard of getting up early to cover it before school.

After getting my BTEC National in business studies, I applied for my first 'proper job'. It was at BT, in Little Park Street. I was 19 and over 2,000 people applied for the job (it was the late 1980s and looking back, good jobs were hard to find), I was one of 40 successful applicants that got a job as a Clerical Officer taking customer service calls in what we now refer to as call centres (I don't think they were established as such back then!). I was one of the youngest staff members of that cohort, with most of the team members being many years older. Whilst working at BT my parents still had their business and if someone called in sick, again, I still did the odd paper round before getting ready for work. It really was just part of living in a small family business. Customers would joke, 'What's the matter? Doesn't BT pay enough?!' Little did I realise, this was a key lesson in customer service, my parents didn't want to let their customers down so did all they could to get the papers delivered, including roping us in!

At the age of 20 my parents thought it was time I got married. So, I was engaged and then married at 21 and moved 'up north'. I went on to have my son at 22 and my daughter at 23 (yes, it was an arranged marriage and no... patience is not one of my strong points!).

During my marriage I worked for varying organisations: I worked in men's retail and went on to be one of the top performers for the store, I worked in politics and during my short time we went from 2 to 11 councillors. I then fell into accounts after covering for a friend, working for a scaffolding company, a large solicitors firm, and in local government. I found all the jobs interesting, however I often got bored and moved on after a couple of years. I always worked part-time to facilitate my children. As a side note, I was also a landlord and managed a number of rental properties, so I guess in reality, I worked full time.

In 2005 my marriage of twelve years came to an abrupt end. So, I decided to move myself and the children 150 miles back to the Midlands, where I had my family and my support system. It was a hard decision, but the right one for us. So, at 33 I found myself divorced with two children and essentially homeless. I had to decide what it was I wanted to do and to take control of my life, so I decided to make a plan.

The aim was in two years to be back in my own home with the income of a two parent family (because this is what the children were used to).

To get me on track, I moved in with my parents, went back to university and did a degree in Business Management. I supported my children through the Grammar School process and began working at Esqué (I was employed there before I became one of the owners).

So, by September 2007 I had:

1. Completed my degree.

2. Moved into my home (I'd built an extension on it to house 5 students to help bring in an additional income).

3. Helped both the children to get into Grammar Schools.

4. Divorced and had custody of the children, after numerous court hearings.

5. Been employed at Esqué for 17 months.

In essence, I had accomplished what I had set out to do. A second valuable lesson, have a plan, then stick to it.

In 2010, I had an opportunity to join the banking industry and was lucky enough to be offered two jobs. I'd now been as Esqué for 4 years and after numerous promotions, felt I'd done all I could at my level for the business. So, with a very heavy heart I handed in my resignation on a Friday. On the following Monday I was asked if I wanted to be a Partner in the business! I certainly was not expecting this at all; I was ready to leave and to try something new but the idea of running the business and being a decision maker really excited me. Coming from a family of business owners (all my siblings work for themselves) it felt right on so many levels. Looking back, I think that's why I'd job hopped so often.

So as they say... the rest is history!

However, I then looked at what I was letting myself into. What was the health of the business when I bought in?

- The business was not not cash rich, we owed on a loan we'd taken out for £100,000 to open the retail space below the salon.

- The company owed a substantial amount in preference shares.

- The treatment menu was extensive and confusing.
- The company was in need of a restructure to be more effective.
- We were holding four times more stock than we needed as a business.
- I had little experience managing a team of 20!

I decided that this presented me with the perfect opportunity to be an amazing boss. Everyone was going to love me. I wasn't going to be THAT kind of boss everyone hated/couldn't stand! My team were going to love me...

So, as you would expect, it didn't happen just like that and it really is a work in progress! Before I share what I have learned, I'll let you know what has been achieved so far:

- The loan has now been cleared.
- The company had paid almost £100,000 in preference shares.
- The treatment menu is now much easier to understand with many peripheral treatments discontinued.
- The salon has won Salon of the Year for the second time.
- We closed the retail space and then reconfigured the therapy space to incorporate retail, a client lounge, and reception, at the same time giving the salon an opulent feel with our change in branding to reflect the 'more'.
- We've reduced our stock holding by 50% and continue to reduce it in accordance to the business needs.
- I took time out to develop myself through various courses and had great support so that I was able to be a better leader in the business. This is ongoing.
- The company introduced an open and honest structure for the team; they can see what the criteria is to get promoted and what they need to do to grow, and they also have a Therapy Manager to support them in their development.
- I created a network of business people around me so that we were able to bounce ideas off one another. Often, it is good

to get a perspective from someone who's not immersed in a challenge that may be causing a headache, they are able to look from the outside in to give a different perspective and help see the situation in a very different light.

So, what did I learn since taking on the business?

- It was ME that needed to grow. I needed to develop to manage the team fairly, confidently, and openly. Myself and my business partner, Amy, have gone on a few day courses together and they definitely helped. I also embarked on a Goldman Sachs course aimed at small businesses wanting to grow.

- I'm still in contact with my cohort and still bounce ideas off them when I'm in a challenge that I'm struggling with, and this has proven to be invaluable. Get a good business community around you; it will save your sanity.

- Know your numbers, be it budgets, stock numbers, or performance. What you don't measure you can't improve.

- Manage change and always present to your team in a way they can understand. It will be better received.

- All businesses have challenges... You are not alone.

- Support your team and show compassion. It goes a long way.

- Teach the 'soft' skills as well as the skills you need in order to do your job. Things like building rapport and 'tell don't sell' to your clients about products and treatments that can genuinely make a difference to them.

- Praise your team regularly and never take them for granted. You are as good as your business and it's your staff that make your business.

- If you do decide to run your own business, make sure you do something you are passionate about as it will test you, and if you don't love it you will stop trying.

So, what's next?

To support my team and the future new talent in my area,

I've become an Industry Advisor for the local college. It's great to discuss how the skills being taught at college are in alignment with what the industry needs.

As part of my development, I've also joined a couple of other boards as a Non-Executive Director. It's a great way of sharing your knowledge and experience with other companies. Essentially most companies have similar challenges; it's rarely industry specific.

I will continue to support and grow the team in the salon, spending most of my time growing my managers, who in turn develop their team members. I love the industry and the people and will stay in it as long as I can.

Gurdip's top tip:

"There are no right or wrong decisions, only lessons to be learned. Cut yourself some slack and try to enjoy the journey. If you can measure something… anything, try, as it will give you a benchmark of how you are doing and help you plan to where you want to be."

Gurdip's favourite quote:

"The sooner you start making mistakes the sooner you can learn what you need to learn to become the success you want to be!"

Gurdip Chatha

www.esquebeauty.com

TWITTER NAME:
@esquebeauty   @GurdipKC

Hannah Alexander

SENIOR BUSINESS MANAGER
LLOYDS BANKING GROUP

"

I HOPE YOU ENJOY READING MY STORY, I
ENJOYED PUTTING IT ON PAPER AS IT GAVE ME
TIME TO REFLECT ON MY CHALLENGES AND MY
ACHIEVEMENTS. HAVING JUST HIT FORTY, IT'S
GOOD TIMING TO THINK ABOUT WHAT MY NEXT
CHAPTER MIGHT LOOK LIKE...

HANNAH ALEXANDER
LLOYDS BANKING GROUP

L et me take you back 25 years to 1993. In some ways it seems like only yesterday, in others it feels like four lifetimes! So, its 1993, I'm 16 and I've just left school where in fact I was Deputy Head Girl (I've still never quite got over not being Head Girl).

Things were going well, and then I met a boy! Maybe if I'd chosen to pay more attention in Biology things might have been different, but as it was I found myself pregnant at 16. This was what you might call my first career hurdle.

Our parents, while shocked, were supportive but the consensus was that we should get married, so we did. It may sound a bit draconian now but I'm a firm believer that things happen for a reason. A year after this I lost my father and I am forever grateful that he got to give me away and meet his first grandchild, Josh. As for the marriage, it didn't last much beyond that, but we remain great friends today.

When Josh was 3 months old I got a job in WH Smiths. I was mainly on the counter selling stationary, newspapers, and lottery tickets (on my CV this is referred to as my early career in Retail!). Whilst there I did an NVQ in customer service, put my hand up for any training course going and by the time I was 18 I was responsible for training all new employees – a role I took very seriously!

After a few years I went to work for Vodafone, again in a customer facing role, and then after that I was approached by an independent telecommunications firm where I got my first experience of managing client relationships.

When I was 25 I saw an advert for a Business Banking Manager for Lloyds Banking Group, the role sounded interesting and I was ready for a change, so I applied. I had mixed emotions when I was offered the role as I thought it was going to be in my local branch, but instead they wanted me to spend the first 12 months in a location that would mean a two hour daily commute. Josh was eight and I was about to get married to the present Mr Alexander. I wasn't sure if I could make it work, but I decided to give it a go.

I guess it must have worked; 15 years later I'm still working for Lloyds Banking Group! On reflection, it was quite a bold move for the bank to offer me the job, at that time there were very few female business managers in the country, certainly none in their early 20s.

After my initial period of training, I returned to Hereford as a Business Manager. I was delighted to be supporting local businesses in my home town. Over the course of 10 years I progressed through the ranks, moving on to support larger clients with more complex needs. I completed my Professional Diploma in Financial Services Management and studied with the Open University. However, it wasn't all plain sailing! Josh had a difficult relationship with school, in fact he went through two primary schools and three secondary schools. This meant I had to work in an agile way, before it became a 'buzz word', and I am grateful that the Bank supported me throughout this time. There was never a question about whether I could leave when there was a crisis at school (sometimes these were daily) and when I needed time off for appointments, I was able to take it. I still got the job done and to a high level. In fact, I probably put more pressure on myself to be delivering as well, if not better, than my peers.

About five years ago I took a sideways move into a training and coaching role. This was a regional role and allowed me to develop new skills and engage some new stakeholders. After about nine months, I was offered the role of Area Director for Coventry & Warwickshire. This was a role that I had been aspiring to for years, but it was 100 miles from home in a location I didn't know, leading a team of people I'd never met. I almost talked myself out of it. Luckily, I had a great boss. He offered me a protected secondment and the opportunity to work flexibly, so I went for it.

In the role I was responsible for leading a team of Relationship Managers who supported around 1000 SME clients. It was clear that the individuals all had great capabilities but collectively they weren't delivering their true potential and performance wasn't where it needed to be. I realised that I needed to galvanise them as a team, create a shared vision, and sense of purpose. Over the course of 24 months our Employee Engagement moved from 59% to 94%, our client satisfaction scores moved from 25 to 40, and we raised £20 000 for local charities. I am really proud of what the team delivered, and I truly believe that if you have happy and motivated colleagues who are connected to the communities that they serve, they will deliver great things for clients. This, in turn, creates the performance outputs that the business needs.

My time in the role wasn't without the odd challenge. Nine months in I had to have an emergency hysterectomy. When the doctors told me I might need up to two months off work I was devastated. However, I was lucky enough to recover quickly and I was back to work after three weeks (no heavy lifting, I promise)!

I mentioned that I did the role as a protected secondment for six months, you'll gather from the above that that was made permanent. I should at this point acknowledge the tremendous and unending support from my husband. I manged to convince him to move from Hereford to Coventry and he subsequently changed jobs. He has supported every decision I have made, he even supported me last year when I signed up for The Fourtitude Challenge. This was a physical challenge that involved climbing the highest peak in England, cycling 100 miles and half marathon. When I signed up I didn't even own a bike, so I spent all my spare time last summer training.

A week before the challenge, I had a call offering me the opportunity to take a new role, working directly with the Managing Director of our SME Business. This was a great opportunity but much like before, timing and location were not ideal and I'll be honest the present Mr Alexander did take a little convincing on this one, having just moved house and changed his job! However, much like before, I decided to give it a go and no sooner had I limped over the line of the half marathon, I was starting a new job in London.

This new role is really varied. It gives me the opportunity to get involved with setting strategy, working with and managing stakeholders from across the bank, and supporting the business to deliver its priorities. It's been a steep learning curve! There have been many times when I have been physically out of my comfort zone, but I really believe that this is when the magic happens!

So, that's me in a nutshell, that's how I went from teenage mum to Senior Leader in the UK's leading bank.

You may be wondering what happened to Josh. Despite his challenging school days, he is forging himself a great career, and at 23 he is in a management position with 50 staff reporting into him and he's currently planning his wedding.

Neither of us had a conventional start in life but I believe that your past doesn't dictate your future. It does help to have great people around you, and through any challenge I have faced I have been lucky to have people on my side being my cheerleader, and so I try and do the same for those around me – the world needs more cheerleaders!

Also, I am lucky to work for a bank that really cares about its people. One of our challenges is that in the Commercial Bank we still have relatively few females in Senior Leadership Roles, something both I and the bank are passionate about changing. Over the years as a female in what was long considered a male domain I have often been in the minority, and there were times when I felt like I couldn't always be myself. However, it is really great to see things changing and it's clear that my organisation values diversity and the benefits that having a diverse organisation brings. I guess it always did – they employed me all those years ago!

Hannah's top tip:

"Don't wait for the perfect time, there isn't one. When an opportunity comes along there is usually something going on that means the timing isn't right. However if you want it, go for it!."

Hannah's favourite quote:

"What have YOU done today to contribute to your happiness and success!"

*I have it on my wall at home
to remind me that my happiness
and success is my responsibility
and no one else's.*

Dr Sharon Redrobe OBE

CEO
TWYCROSS ZOO (EAST MIDLAND ZOOLOGICAL SOCIETY)

"

I REALLY BELIEVE YOU CAN DO ANYTHING YOU SET
YOUR MIND TO – BUT NO ONE EVER SAID IT WOULD
BE EASY. THE JOURNEY MAY BE SHORT OR LONG,
AND WHO KNOWS IF YOU'RE THERE YET, BUT I LOVE
DOING WHAT I'M DOING NOW AND THAT INCLUDES
CONSTANTLY CHANGING TOO. OF COURSE, IT'S
IMPORTANT FOR SUCCESS TO BE ABLE TO WORK HARD,
STUDY HARD, AND BE AN EXPERT IN WHAT YOU DO,
BUT DON'T FORGET TO LOOK AFTER YOUR HEART
AND SOUL TOO – GETTING THAT WORK/LIFE BALANCE
RIGHT IS TRICKY AND PROBABLY MY HARDEST LESSON.
I BELIEVE I'M GETTING THERE NOW.

DR SHARON REDROBE OBE // TWYCROSS ZOO

DR SHARON REDROBE OBE
TWYCROSS ZOO

"Do or do not. There is no try", says Yoda to a frustrated Luke Skywalker in Star Wars. This has pretty much been the theme of my life. I'm the now the CEO of Twycross Zoo and very proud to be running a world class charity zoo with around 200 employees, making a healthy surplus from £12M turnover, and caring for over 500 rare animals, after turning it around from a failing business losing £1M a year, quite dreadful staff morale, and chimpanzees in ancient enclosures.

I believe it's very important to have role model, mine is Jane Goodall. Jane went out to Africa as a young woman in the 1960s. As a 'mere woman' she achieved a scientific breakthrough (gaining a PhD without doing a degree first), gained the trust of wild chimpanzees for the first time when others thought it impossible, stood up against the establishment, and has moved on to tour the world lecturing 300 days a year to try and save the forest and the chimps.

Chimpanzees, science, and saving the planet is therefore what I wanted to do for the rest of my life after reading her books as a 12 year old - but then reality hit. Especially after I spoke to my school career officer about being a wildlife vet and he said, 'Not really, love, you are a 5'2" female – apply to law or medicine.' Telling me 'no' is probably the best way to get me motivated! I applied to all the Universities that taught veterinary medicine two years later and got into the London University Royal Veterinary College when it was still very much a male dominated profession. These days it is very different, now when I lecture in vet schools over 60% of the intake is female. It was an open secret at vet school that I was a 'lost cause' to traditional vet work as my heart was set on zoo and wildlife work. I spent most of my holidays in USA or UK zoos or wildlife centres. Scraping by most exams, I applied myself to the social and political aspects of University as being on a vet degree meant I spent six years in London. I ended my University life as Student Union President.

A few months before graduation I was looking through the Vet Record at the job ads knowing that 'wildlife' jobs would be like hen's teeth, when I saw 'vet wanted to start the zoo and wildlife programme at Edinburgh University and be the zoo vet at Edinburgh zoo - five years experience required'. As I'd been at vet school for five years, I feel I blagged my way into the interview process; I talked about my USA wildlife training and landed the job! I set up the first UK programme for wildlife vets and within a few years I had passed my post graduate examinations to become a Specialist, was running an exotic pet and a rabbit clinic, alongside covering Edinburgh Zoo, I was being invited to lecture all over Europe and USA, and had authored several academic books and papers. The travel and conference parties were fun, but after six years I was getting bored!

Bristol Zoo began recruiting for their own vet department for the first time in its 175 year history so of course I applied. I finally got to go to Africa to provide vet care to the chimpanzee rescue centre based in Cameroon. Not quite saving the world (yet!) but that started my 20-year association with Ape Action Africa.

At Bristol, I was promoted into the management team. I loved doing vet work but wanted to do more and look at the bigger picture strategically and be involved with running the whole business. While at Bristol I got involved with strategic planning for the existing 15-acre zoo in the city, plus development planning for a new 100-acre new zoo park just outside of Bristol. This provided great training for me on so many levels. Typical project challenges happened along the way; dealing with species specialists, architects, engineers, 'value engineering', and a multitude of consultants. This was all an exciting learning curve and rather like herding cats! In the midst of this I felt my biological clock ticking and so I had my only son. The Zoo had never dealt with a senior member of staff getting pregnant, nor coming back when lactating(!); I had far too many excruciating meetings with the old guy that did Health and Safety and the HR people assuming I'd never work again. I actually continued working until the Friday and had Jake on the Wednesday, and after a few weeks dealing with phone calls and the odd on-site visit, went back to work almost on-the-dot at six months.

And yet... I was getting itchy feet again. The University of Nottingham was starting the first new UK vet school for over 50 years, were actively head hunting me, and had a USP that they were going to work with their local zoo and embed it the programme, which I would manage. So, I thought yes, I'll come and do that for ten years or so, I'll be a Professor and get involved with strategic planning at a University level and that will enhance my CV to become a CEO of an animal charity or better still, charitable zoo, some day. The ten-year plan didn't work out as it was a mere two years before I was taking up the role of CEO of Twycross Zoo (TZ).

TZ was founded in 1963, specialising in breeding and rearing monkeys and apes, and also training chimpanzees for TV work. In 2004 the founders, and chimps, retired and the now charity zoo was then governed by a board of trustees and its first CEO. Less than ten years later, the zoo was losing money culminating in a £1M loss in the year 2012. By this time, I'd made it my 'hobby' to analyse what made zoos successful across Europe and USA; I'd visited many and was increasingly interested in the running of the whole zoo 'business'. Given the laudable improvements in animal welfare driving larger and more expensive enclosures, I'd predicted zoos would be facing a crisis of funding and management. I passionately felt one didn't have to 'sell your soul' and over-commercialise the operation; the zoo could and should put animals at the heart of what it was doing, but equally making money was essential to the achievement of those noble aims. I was desperate to run a charity zoo, not only adequately to cover the costs of animal care and conservation, but financially successful and world class.

I was advising on business turnaround from a zoological

perspective to the then TZ Board which had recognised that a major shift of its fortunes was required. They had identified the need for a new senior team and were indeed looking for a business professional with extensive turnaround experience for the role. I eventually successfully argued that zoos, and working with animals, is only likely to get more expensive and challenging, running a zoo despite the apparently 'small' turnover is actually a complex mixture of operations, animal welfare, legislation, construction, and education and I had the vision to pull all that together (if not yet the hard-commercial experience from Plc-land).

Basically, I feel I blagged my way into another job - though to be fair, I believe many women say this too much so I should stop - I had actually developed quite a unique skill set, and worked very hard, to get myself into a position to apply for such a role.

In October 2013, one week after my birthday, I finally got the hot seat, but then had a sinking feeling. I was now the boss of something that was losing huge amounts of money relative to turnover, hadn't seen growth for many years, with really high overheads and a disgruntled body of staff, falling visitor numbers, and a lack of investment, meaning most of the buildings were in dire need of renovation. That's fine, I'm thinking, I'm a good person, a good leader, or about to be (after all, I'd been on several leadership courses, read lots of books, and watched lots of TED talks...), and everyone would love me once I demonstrated all the things I'd read and learned about, and it will be fine... oh, how naïve. I now know having thick skin is an essential element of leadership!

So, TZ is the only zoo in the UK and one of very few in the world that has the whole set of apes - gorilla, bonobo, chimpanzee and orang-utan. I immediately made TZ members of the UN programme GRASP (great ape survival partnership), which was created when the UN agreed that great apes will all be extinct in the wild within 20 years. I finally got to meet my hero Jane Goodall for a coffee in London to discuss this, and whether she'd support our masterplan relaunch (she did!). She's actually very supportive of zoos these days (those that are managed well) as she's seen chimps in the wild hurt and killed by poachers, and knows full well the role that decent zoos now play.

I began my tenure as CEO writing a business plan, of course. But this one could not just be a short term three-year plan; in my mind it had to address the failing infrastructure and restructure all the costs in order to show we knew how to manage the 'business' side of the zoo and gain major investment. We had less than half a million visitors a year, and this figure was falling (but still made us one of the UK's most visited zoos), yet we had a 35-acre zoo on an 88-acre plot, with up to 10,000 people visiting on some (infrequent) days - so why not more people more often? I commissioned market research and focus groups; I needed to challenge the status quo.

In the first six months, we wrote a five-year business plan with a 20-year vison. Using all-staff workshops to gather ideas, it became apparent that reshaping our site into a modern zoo would take over £55M and maybe 20 years of rebuilding. Figures that should have scared me but, perhaps naïvely, I felt it was 'just a matter of money and time' as we had an outstanding site, location, and animal collection, so I took the plan to banks to seek loans to kick-start the zoo. I was almost laughed out of the first room by a group of bankers who felt it was their role to tell me how risky this was; the business had been losing money for too long and I should just reshape it into a much smaller affordable farm park, or better still just close it. 'How rude!', I thought.

Within weeks I had two other banks in meetings quizzing me about the potential revenue, overheads, net profit, operating profit, EBITDA, debt servicing levels, etc., etc. How quickly I'd transformed from a monkey vet to talking business turnaround! In the midst of these negotiations, I changed Financial Directors (twice) and Marketing Directors. Eyebrows were raised but I explained I needed rapidly changing skill sets and appetite, and somewhat to my surprise the banks stayed on board. Later one of the bank team told me that backers buy into the passion and vision of the CEO, not necessarily the whole team, and they actively appreciate leadership decisions such as the ones I was making. At the time, I had other advice strongly advising me to not even try, and much less not to change the team too soon, advice I continue to cheerfully ignore.

I've widened TZ thinking to not just think about saving wildlife (vital, of course!), but also to be seen as a proper business. I encouraged staff to apply for as many awards as possible to 'shine their light' and I'm delighted to say we've been awarded many; for our staff, our animal welfare advances, and our business turnaround. Together with my excellent HR director, we established a whole culture change programme. Not just in words and workshops, but truly pulling and guiding all the staff to appreciate that to turn around TZ, we needed to change attitudes. Some didn't get this at all; 'but we've always done it like this', or, 'that won't work, love', were constant challenges in the staff group meetings. There was so little understanding of working in teams, and although I was delighted to see many women in junior roles, the sex ratio became depressingly male further up the ranks.

Many people had never worked at or even visited another zoo and were wide eyed when I actively not only encouraged this, but set up trips (during work time for which they got paid!) to visit other places and learn the best practices. Of course, there were those that felt they already knew best and I was just a 'young thing' that would soon leave. A turning point for me was when one older chap, who'd been at the zoo 'in the good old days' told me that girls couldn't work on his area or he'd resign. There was much spluttering when I took him up on his offer. Likewise, two women, much older than me, ran one area of the zoo as a personal fiefdom, failing to upskill new employees so many either left or quickly became infected with the same 'things never change, management are evil' mind-set. Others knew 'who to talk to to get things done', often undermining managers or openly badmouthing others. Some staff relished the new open culture – I have an open-door policy but equally expect them to discuss issue with their line managers first, it's respectful at the very least.

I cannot say it's been easy. I've had to develop a very thick skin to those that felt I was changing TZ for the worse - staff and long-term members included (you should see the emails, and even closely written 12 page letters I've had!), but I believe the results now speak for themselves. Visitor numbers have grown by 25%, and we make our own cash for developments, having invested over £8M in the site in the last five years - only half of which was a bank loan in the end.

We outsourced several divisions - catering, marketing, maintenance, horticulture – calling on expertise that others could bring in order for these areas to make money (or in the case of maintenance and horticulture, cost less and be better skilled!), as we needed to focus on our core job of running the zoo. We kept retail in house as it was making money. Eyebrows were raised when I let go of most of the 'commercial' department staff but the stark truth was they weren't making enough money. I spent time in various lunchtimes, staff rooms, and offices, explaining to all staff that we need to make money, and lose less, so the monkeys could have better facilities and the public would visit. Although the first developments were animal-related (butterfly house, lemur walk through, giraffes and gibbons), I also spent large sums on toilets, paths and children's play areas; it was crucial for me to bring the staff with me on understanding that we had to improve customer satisfaction so we could bring in the money to fund the animal areas. All the animal staff of course talk to the public, and their buy-in and attitude was essential to the success of our turnaround. People find change unsettling, and staff turnover and changes were often called out as negative, whereas I wanted to encourage a change in attitude; staff leaving for promotion elsewhere, and indeed fresh blood and ideas arriving, were positives.

Now staff morale, based on the anonymous surveys we do every year, is at an all-time high. I even get scored individually (the only team member to so do) and these results are published for all the staff to see.

A couple of years ago I was approached to apply for Business Woman of the Year. I felt if nothing else it would be good experience to be grilled by top business people; as of course they wouldn't think it's a proper business, or that I'm up to much 'real' business. I was genuinely stunned when I was handed the engraved rose bowl by Karren Brady herself. And although this story sounds like I'm full of self-confidence, it took that moment to realise that actually

I'd always had a little voice in my head saying I was blagging my way through life and was about to be found out... it turns out some people actually do think I know what I'm doing!

I've since been flying the flag for women in business, having judged other business awards, sat on local LEP and CBI Boards, and been especially delighted to be a judge for Woman Who... and to be part of seeing other women transformed by being recognised and encouraged. Last year, I was humbled to receive an OBE for my work with tourism and conservation. My personal life has finally dropped into place too, meeting the love of my life at a business event. What a journey. I feel like it's just starting...

Sharon's top tip:

"Overall to lead change and make a difference I think you need a combination of belief in your vision, willingness to constantly improve and adapt, and a thick skin. I've eventually learned to 'not sweat the small stuff'; when there's lots to do you can get swamped in detail but it really is even more essential to then take a step back and 'work on the business, not in the business'. Take the time at least once a month to think and reset. Above all, be honest with yourself and others; this truly is the key to good leadership. It's about treating everyone fairly and honestly, even when (actually, especially when) it's difficult to do so. Business really is about people and money. Probably in that order."

Sharon's favourite quotes:

"Do or do not. There is no try."
Yoda, Star Wars

"Gonna live while I'm alive and sleep when I'm dead."
Bon Jovi

"Only if we understand will we care. Only if we care will we help. Only if we help shall all be saved."
Dame Jane Goodall

www.twycrosszoo.org

TWITTER NAME:
@Spr1969

Helen Walbey

DIRECTOR
RECYCLE SCOOTERS

"

DON'T GIVE UP, EVEN WHEN THE GOING GETS
TOUGH, AS YOU ARE STRONGER THAN YOU THINK.
IF MY JOURNEY INTO BUSINESS CAN HELP YOU FIND
SOME LIGHT IN THE DARK THEN I THANK YOU FOR
THE TIME YOU HAVE TAKEN TO READ IT.

HELEN WALBEY
RECYCLE SCOOTERS

I accidentally fell into running a business with no previous experience or idea on how I was going to make it succeed, but within two years I had taken my pub from the bottom of a league table of fifty establishments to third. Not bad for a local village pub that only opened in the evenings and didn't serve food, especially considering we were competing with establishments in Cardiff and Bristol city centre.

I did it through a combination of damned hard work and learning how to listen; I listened to what my customers wanted and built strategic ideas, events, and products that they would love; I listened to suppliers and kept on top of the latest trends and took advantage of special offers and extra training; I listened to my staff, as they were the ones who knew my customers best; I listened to professional experts like my accountant, business support services, and my solicitor, who saved me about £12,000 on my Lease by suggesting re-wording one small paragraph. I spent twice as much time listening and learning as I did talking and teaching, and I filtered all the advice and information I received. I double checked it, tried out new ideas, and discovered how to make a business grow. The three-year business loan was repaid in ten months, and life was good.

Due to structural problems our pub had to close for major refurbishment/rebuilding work and we had the chance to take on three others and really grow our business. However, I had been listening to the industry and to the news and I knew a smoking ban was coming, I also knew the economy was due to continue the cycle and crash in the not too distant future, so I listened to my gut feeling and took my capital and moved onto a new project. Business is about taking risks, but those risks have to be balanced.

With my experience to shield me, my husband and I commissioned a custom-made food trailer so we could start indulging our passion for food and supplying vegetarian, vegan, and organic food at events up and down the country. In 2002 this was a new idea for many of the events we attended and we were incredibly busy. I was working with my husband who, after 24 years, is still my best friend. We were serving food we loved to great people; customers who loved it just as much as we did. No-one saw that disaster was about to strike and we were totally unprepared for what happened next.

My husband, Steve, got a tiny burn on his right middle finger. He cleaned and plastered it and we thought nothing more of it. The next morning, he had a fat, bright pink, sausage looking finger. It was the last day of the event so we served breakfast, cleaned down the trailer and van, and headed to the minor injuries unit on the way home. We had not noticed the small red line that started to creep up his arm. I was anticipating coming away with a short course of antibiotics for Steve and so I was taken aback and frightened to be told he needed to have his hand operated on there and then.

The one red line turned into four and they started to move up his arm at a faster rate. Steve's temperature went up and up and then he was moved to the specialist plastic surgery unit in Morriston Hospital, Swansea. He stayed there for the next six weeks whilst they initially battled to save his life, and then his hand and arm. Thanks to amazing NHS care, Steve came home with all his fingers and toes. His right hand does not work as well as it should but it was a small price to pay to see him recover.

The large price I paid was the £144,000 I then owed for not going to work for a month, forfeiting all the deposits we had paid for events, and instead staying at the hospital hoping my most favourite person in the world would get better. The bank put our account on stop, we then sold the trailer, the fridge van, the car, my motorbikes, Steve's motorbikes, and then everything else in the house bar the bed, the books, and the dog. We did not need the appliances as by this point we had had the gas and electric disconnected and the whole place was four degrees. It was November and I have never, ever been as cold in my life as I was that winter. Getting a job was not an option as I would never be able to repay all the money. I desperately did not want to declare myself bankrupt and lose the house, so we came up with a plan. Another business.

It may or may not have been a great plan, but I will never know because as we were testing the idea and seeing if the business might work, we needed money to eat, so we were selling all the motorcycle parts we had accumulated over the years. We then saw a job lot of parts for £750 but had no money to buy them. After not being quite honest with my father and father in law they each gave us £375 and we had the capital to buy the parts. We had no way of collecting them so roped a friend with a van to go to Gatwick from South Wales to help us collect everything. We had no money to pay him but I cook a mean curry so for two weeks he ate like a king and we became the owner of a huge pile of motorcycle parts and accessories. Much head scratching and consternation ensued whilst I tried to figure out what they fitted and where they went on various bikes and scooters. I managed to get a bigger company to take all the Honda parts off our hands for £500, so I bought a bike that didn't work and got Steve to teach me how to fix it. He couldn't do the work due to the damage in his hand, but he had the knowledge so once again I sat, I listened, and I learnt. I learnt enough to mend the bike I bought for £100 and sold it for £400. I then bought another bike.

That was the start of our second unintended business. Each time I sold something, I paid a tiny bit of the debt back and bought another bike/scooter or box of parts. Each time I repaired a bike, I learnt a new skill. Eventually I bought a bike that I could not repair. I was about to lose all my profit margin so decided instead to see if I could sell in in parts instead. That dismantling job was the start of Recycle Scooters Ltd. 14 years later we have a team of four staff, two small industrial units, our bike purchases are lorry loads of about 80 machines at a time, and we ship all over the world. I never thought I would be running a business like this but here we are, still getting bigger, and still enjoying it.

The last 14 years have been hard, trying to pay back all the money, going through the financial crash of 2008, and now the vote for Brexit. At one point we had 54 motorcycle top boxes stacked up next to the bed in our bedroom and for years all the exhausts, forks, and swing arms lived in the spare room. We converted the dining room into a home office, built a 25 metre workshop in the garden and filled that with parts, then built another one and filled that too. In 2014 we finally outgrew the house and realised full blown industrial premises were the next logical step. We moved over 20 ton of equipment and stock over the Easter weekend aided by some amazing friends, our work van, and a lot of curry and beer. As soon as the couriers were back working after the Easter break, our parcels were going back out. A customer would not even have known we had moved sites.

During that time, I learnt to adapt, to not give up, and still to keep listening. I wanted to focus on motorcycles but my customers kept asking for small capacity machines and scooters, so now that is where most of our trade comes from. eBay customers wanted me to be able to ship to them all over the world, so we now work with about four different courier firms so we can get almost anything we sell shipped almost anywhere on the globe. We recycle all our plastic, metal, fluid, and paper waste - we even have a compost bin for the food waste and a dog for the scraps. In the true spirt of recycling, Big Dog was once a dumped dog and we rescued him for another chance at life. We respond to all our international customers in the language they enquire in, so I have taken French lessons and we use translation services to help us. Our international enquiry to sale conversion rate is excellent.

The business presents new challenges every day; it is hard physically and very dirty, although much of this we clean up and decontaminate regularly. The industry itself is still totally male dominated and has some very backward attitudes and business practices in place. Nude calendars are still something I see all too often, even now. Being a physically small woman in such a macho world has certainly presented me with a few difficult situations and some challenging conversations but I have dealt with them all with a thick skin and a good sense of humour. I have, however, always

- and I mean always - called people out. Most aggression and hate stems from fear, so by calling out wrongdoing and helping to educate others, I have built a positive reputation in the industry as someone who is honest and fair to deal with, but takes no rubbish and is not a pushover. At the start of my business journey I paid more for the bikes than I do now but I have never changed the way to do business; I have just become more skilled at negotiating. Now I know when to walk away from a contract if it is not a good deal. I am much better at saying no and understanding my own value and moral worth, as some business is just not worth having.

I try to ensure that I support others constantly, so all our team have the opportunity to undertake any workplace learning they feel is relevant to their role, whether that be a full-blown apprenticeship, or a short online first aid course. This resulted in my business advisor berating me for leading the ship from the back and not undertaking any professional development or learning myself. I hated university when I was lucky enough to go as an 18 year old, I didn't complete my degree and had no desire to repeat any of the experience. But, with a lot of cajoling and a European Social Fund funded course I undertook a two-year foundation degree in Business and Enterprise. I don't like failing, so I again listened, I learnt about the topics, but more importantly I learnt the rules of the game. I learnt how to write academic essays; I understood the pattern and got straight distinctions for my course. I then undertook a Post Graduate Diploma in Gendered Entrepreneurship Practice and I learnt so much about the theory around women in business. This gave me real context alongside my many years of practice. I thought things were difficult for me because I was in such a male dominated industry; it was only when I went on this course that my eyes were really opened to the full reality of being a woman in business. Being white and able bodied I face much less discrimination than others, so I also had to learn about and acknowledge the privilege I have, and then work in ways to dismantle unfair structures and working practices. It is not equality until we all have equal opportunities. I gave some guest lectures at the university and was encouraged to think about a career change and move into academia; so, I then undertook Post Graduate Teacher training. I eventually graduated with three distinctions in four years. All I did was work and study. Steve worked, cooked, cleaned, ran baths, and occasionally took my books off me and made me stop. I have no idea if I could do it again now and I certainly couldn't have done it without him, but I learnt what it is possible to achieve if we put our minds to it. I have lectured at the University of South Wales, part time, for the last four years but being an entrepreneur is still more fun than being an academic, so I never did make the leap.

I started listening to discussions about business policy and how it affects businesses owned and led by women, I started asking questions and reading more. The more I listened, the more I got told, the more I learnt. The more I learnt, the more I wanted to be part of the change in making business opportunities equal to everyone, regardless of gender, religion, race, sexuality, age, or disability. I got involved with the university's Women in Enterprise hub (where I am now an ambassador), I signed up as a mentor with Virgin Start Up, which involves mentoring one new business each year. I was approached by the Welsh Government to become a role model for school children and young people in college or university, which involved going out and telling people about my scrap yard and how I overcame all the challenges. Being a Big Ideas Role Model and inspiring the next generation to start their own businesses and to follow their dreams is the best feeling.

I then noticed that when I went to events, awards, or networking it was virtually always all male. I started speaking up and pushing for more alternative options/speakers/ themes. I got a lot of push back but I kept going. I was appointed as the Federation of Small Businesses' first Diversity and Health Policy Portfolio Chair, looking after small businesses across the U.K. If you want to go fast, go alone, but if you want to go far, go together. There are now 14 people on the Women in Enterprise taskforce in the FSB, we have a LGBT+ working group and specific activities to support, engage, and listen to ethnic minority entrepreneurs and all our younger FSB members. There is still the opportunity to do so much more. My role is to be available, to listen, and learn before I think, and then do.

My role with the FSB has taken me to 10 Downing Street with a delegation of 20 women to discuss business policy, it has led me to give evidence in the Welsh Parliament, and share a stage with Nicola Mendelsohn, the Vice president of Facebook EMA, when we launched the U.K. leg of the #SheMeansBusiness campaign, of which the FSB are one of the key partners. I am no superwoman, I am just an ordinary business woman from the top of the South Wales Valleys who wants to make a positive difference. Any one of us can do the same thing.

If ten years ago someone had said to me that I would be doing half the things I do now, I would never have believed them, but it is amazing what we can achieve with an open mind, hard work, and an ability to know our own worth. I love what I do; I meet some amazing, inspiring women just like you who have great businesses, while also juggling homes, children, parents, and attempting to have a social life. I am regularly astounded by the incredible stories I hear and the power, patience, and passion women across the land show to their businesses, communities, and tribes.

If you are thinking, should I? Then yes, you should. If you are thinking, can I? Then yes, you can, and you can find other to help you. If you are thinking, how will I? Then you are ready to listen, to ask questions, to plan, to dream, and most of all to not put it off until tomorrow. You never know what the future will hold so don't miss out on your dreams; make your dreams a reality with all the blood, sweat, tears, laughter, and cake that is required to turn your business into a successful, sustainable, and fun place to be.

I wish you all the very best of luck in whatever you choose to do and thank you for reading my story about a scrap yard in Wales, born from a disaster, but still fuelled by love and passion every day.

Helen's top tip:

"Don't go it alone. Your strength lies in those you surround yourself with; the power of your network. If you need help, seek it out and ask for it - it strengthens you personally and supports you professionally. You might be the figurehead of what you do but it is all the people who have your back that will give you the resilience to carry on and the determination to succeed. There is also nothing wrong in saying 'no' or walking away from things that don't feel right, as your gut instinct is rarely wrong.

The right mentor can be invaluable so read all that you can, talk with everyone, and learn to listen well. A mentor does not need to be someone 'superhuman', just someone who can help you to the next stage of your professional and business development. Finding the right one can make all the difference, so choose well."

Helen's favourite quote:

"Fear is the path to the dark side. Fear leads to anger, anger leads to hate, and hate leads to suffering."

Yoda

www.recyclescooters.co.uk

TWITTER NAME:
@RecycleScooters

Holly Matthews

ACTRESS | VLOGGER | POSITIVE MINDSET COACH | SPEAKER
THE HAPPY ME PROJECT

"

FOR THOSE OF YOU READING THIS BOOK, IF
MY MESSAGE CONNECTS WITH YOU, THEN LET'S
CONNECT. I WOULD LOVE TO SEE YOU AT ONE OF MY
WORKSHOPS OR TO HEAR ABOUT YOUR IDEAS. KNOW
THAT WHATEVER YOU ARE GOING THROUGH RIGHT
NOW WILL PASS. TAKE CHARGE OF YOUR LIFE.
I BELIEVE IN YOU WITH ALL MY HEART AND TRUST
THAT EVERYTHING YOU ARE GOING THROUGH WILL
ENABLE YOU TO GROW AND TAKE YOU WHERE YOU
NEED TO BE (EVEN IF IT DOESN'T FEEL LIKE IT RIGHT
NOW). THANK YOU FOR YOUR SUPPORT AND LOVE,
AND LET'S ALL MAKE THIS YEAR A FABULOUS ONE.

HOLLY MATTHEWS
THE HAPPY ME PROJECT

At age 11 I answered the phone to a UK television company and was given the news that they had written a character for me into one of their award winning children's TV shows and my life was about to change.

To most this would have been jaw dropping, but to me it felt the natural next step in my life journey. I had utter belief in myself and if you had spoken to me at this age I'd have introduced myself as, 'Hi, I'm Holly and I'm an actress', way before I actually was.

I grew up in Newcastle Upon Tyne in a working-class home full of love. My Dad, Brian, was a welder who spent time working on oil rigs and my Mum, Clare, worked in a bank. No one in my family came from the entertainment industry and yet here I was suddenly beginning my dream job and bringing in money at only 11 years old. I had no idea how this would change the course of my life.

I got this part by writing a letter to the production team, which I now have on a canvas as a reminder that I must always ask for what I want. In Newcastle we have a saying that goes 'shy bairns, get nowt!' (shy children get nothing!), and in my very talkative, open family, you have to speak up to get heard. I was taught to make myself known.

I truly had no idea back then that this would be exactly how my life would go. That even now, at 33, I am still doing exactly the same thing. Once it's a thought in my head, I speak up, I jump in, and I work it out afterwards. Thankfully that seems to work for me.

I grew up on TV, playing the part of Emma Miller for seven years on UK children's drama, Byker grove, which at the time was watched by millions. Towards the end of the seven years my character on the show had begun a singing career and like life imitating art, I had been approached by Sony and had been secretly recording material, ready for leaving the show.

As a singer I did the rounds of TV channels such as MTV, Disney, Nickelodeon, and the iconic UK show, Top of the Pops. I travelled the UK appearing at clubs and on radio shows, springing up in every major newspaper and magazine in the UK.

Life seemed easy.

The music industry was vastly changing though and with the rise of music talent shows such as Pop Idol, record labels no longer nurtured their talent. It was top ten or you were out.

My first single bounced in at 32 in the UK charts and on the Monday after it went out on Radio 1's chart show, I took a call to say, 'Thanks, it's been great working with you and good luck.'

Woah?!?!

Suddenly, I realised that things don't always go to plan. I hadn't ever considered this before. Life had seemed simple and this was a huge blow, but also the best lesson I could ever have had.

Over the next year I was back to basics, I was auditioning for TV shows and films and travelling from Newcastle to London every week on the train. It was costing me a fortune and the money I had saved from my time in Byker Grove was being whittled away. I worked two jobs, one in a cafe and one at a museum, but was narrowly missing major roles every week. So, I decided I need to go to drama school and move to London.

After auditioning for the best drama schools in the country I was offered a place at the prestigious East 15 Acting School.

At drama school I realised that if I wanted to act I had to make money. Acting can be an expensive business and I had never been a poor actor. But being at drama school there was little room to work and I started my first steps into entrepreneurship.

I printed off flyers and walked my local area handing them out and pushing them through people's doors. I offered myself up as a cleaner, babysitter, and admin help. I cleaned houses, I worked at a psychologist's house, typing for him in his shed office as he dictated the book he was writing (a job my Dad begged me to stop doing!), and I worked as a waitress in a strip club.

During the holidays of drama school, I learnt about promotional modelling and I found a new way to work around what I really wanted to do. This meant I spent my weekends giving out chocolate bars, dressed as a yoghurt, smiling in cocktail dresses, and selling alcohol at prestigious parties. I enjoyed this way of working; it was good fun, made me very good money, and developed my confidence.

I was still auditioning while at drama school (although this was definitely not allowed) and two weeks before finishing my first year I left. I had been offered a major role in one of the most popular TV shows in the UK at the time, Waterloo Road. It was worth the risk and I packed a bag and headed to Manchester, back to the north.

After finishing Waterloo Road I bounced around from TV shows (The Bill, Doctors, Casualty) to film roles and even worked as a CBEEBIES radio presenter. I worked fairly consistently and although I was still doing promotional work I made the bulk of my money from acting and modelling.

Alongside acting and entertainment work I was always coming up with ways to make money that worked around auditions and acting and when I met my husband, Ross, he taught me how to make 'me' into a business and I began to take my brand seriously.

Just a few of the business ventures I have embarked on (not all successfully) include teaching an adult acting class, Imapregnantmodel.com (used during both of my pregnancies), The Headshot Doctor (an actors' headshot company), teaching people confidence techniques, organising girls and boys selling shots in bars across Essex, and helping to launch a reality TV show.

As an actor I had always worked on my mindset, having to take rejection after rejection, regardless of success, can take its toll on anyone and so I was heavily into self-development.

At 26 I became a mum for the first time to baby Brooke, born six weeks early due to pre-eclampsia, and two years later my second daughter, Texas, came into the world.

By then I had several revenue streams: acting, teaching, speaking, writing, modelling, and working with brands, and our lives as a family were pretty brilliant.

Then in 2014 our world changed.

'I'm sorry Mr Blair, but you have a brain tumour. We will do what we can but if we cannot help we will just make you comfortable.' The words rang in my ears and I felt like I was being sucked into the floor.

Ross just said, *'OK, what's next?'*

Our life was about to take a very different turn.

I phoned my agent. I'd been booked to shoot a film, playing a footballer's wife and was to begin filming that week.

Not now.

I told my agent I didn't want to work and turned my attention to my family.

Brain surgeries, chemotherapy, radiotherapy followed. Doctors appointments, injections, pills, and a shift in roles for us as a couple.

Our lives were changed.

I changed.

I can vividly remember coming home from the hospital on my own for perhaps the first time since we had been told that it was grade four, rare, and he had 50/50 chance of surviving five years. I sat on my kitchen floor and sobbed. I cried for what felt like forever; really ugly cries. Then suddenly I had more clarity than I had ever had before. I realised in that moment that if I wanted to be happy, it was me that was going to have to make that happen, and I decided that I would do whatever it took to get me and my family through this period in our lives.

Then I took stock, I looked at what I wanted for my life and I brought my work closer to home. I initially started a network marketing company, built a successful team and made a very decent amount of money around my family, but after a short time I realised that this way of working wasn't for me and I was very burnt out.

I did, however, learn some very valuable business lessons. I also realised that in network marketing my interest was never the products, it was always the people I coached. I enjoy the development of people and helping to unlock their potential.

So once again I stopped, looked at my life, and shook it up once more. You should never be scared to do this. You don't have to be one thing forever; move and adapt, wherever and whenever you need to.

I spent about three months in a very low period of my life, that I now see as my transitional time.

During this time of stopping I realised that my love of self-development, entrepreneurship and people had already combined to build my own personal brand and I just had to develop that.

I hired a personal business coach, Rebecca Bardess, and I got to work. This fabulous lady injected some life back into me and reminded me of who I am. I will be forever grateful for that.

SOMETIMES YOU NEED COACHES AND MENTORS TO GUIDE YOU!

During this down time (which didn't look like down time to anyone else), I dug deep into who I am and what I wanted. I had to stop playing it safe and just be myself completely, those that liked that would come and those that didn't, simply weren't my people.

My own brand of *'no bullshit self-development'* was truly born.

I invested heavily in myself so that I could be the best for others. I got back to doing things I love. I began writing, reading, learning again, and filling my time with positivity.

I learnt about the online marketing world and began developing business and mindset courses people could buy. I developed a revenue stream that meant once I had done the work I could continue earning, even in my sleep. This excited me.

My husband's health was largely pretty good at this time and although the cancer was always in the background, we lived a happy life. My coaching practice soared and I was also asked to become a paid vlogger for Channel Mum, an ITV affiliate and fantastic network of women. I was nominated for awards for my YouTube channel, 'Holly Matthews Online', where I talked about my life and positive mindset, and I had brands contacting me to work with me.

I became a high-profile supporter of The Brain Tumour Charity and talked openly about the realities of our life.

I launched my first major online self-development course, with a psychologist friend, Caroline Hardwick, called The Bossing it! Academy. Bossing it! is a law of attraction course, for those that like straight talking self-development and it quickly gained some a lot of exposure. We had celebrities, influencers, and household names through our virtual doors and were featured on the BBC and in The Daily Mirror.

Things were on the up, opportunities were flowing in.

Then in July 2017 my husband died.

It felt sudden.

My world broke.

I changed again.

We had spent a wonderful holiday in Turks and Caicos and on our return Ross had a seizure and began to deteriorate.

It was quick; brutal, and I spent a month living in a hospice with him. Nothing prepares you for that, the pain of watching the life drain from a man you adore, a man whose soul was so full of life it impacted everyone around him.

Everyone rallied round, the support was incredible.

I talked openly about what was going on and drew strength from the knowledge that my authentic living could help others live their truth too.

In my time in the hospice I mediated daily, focused on gratitude, and detached from the reality of what was happening next to me. I worked on my business, wrote, completed modules of a course I was doing, even selling online positivity products from his bedside. I also helped raise over £11,000 for the hospice that gave my husband such a dignified end of life.

I needed to learn from what was happening and knowing exactly the entrepreneurial fireball my husband was, and his very black and white attitude to life and death, I knew what he would want me to do. This may seem strange to those on the periphery, but the likelihood is that most of mine and Ross' life would have seemed strange to the majority.

I am now nearly six months on from his death as I write this and although the pain is deep, there are also beautiful things happening in mine and my family's life too.

During my time in the hospice I sought out those that had walked the path in front of me. People who had also gone through tough stuff but were able to soar. I didn't want to see people who are a wreck; I wanted to see positivity, strength and hope. Society often wants to squeeze us into a box, and when it comes to grief and loss we expect a certain decorum and we want people to play the grieving widower.

I am not a victim and knowing I was losing my best friend has driven me to appreciate life in a way I couldn't fathom before.

Since Ross died, I have allowed myself to be. If I want to cry, I cry. If I want to laugh, I laugh, and it's all OK.

I have spent my last few months developing my newest online self-development course, The Happy Me Project. This is 21 days of positivity, audios, videos, a workbook, and everything you need to kick start your mindset.

I wanted it to reach the wide audience that had watched my life for the past eight months as my husband's death played out in the UK press. I want those people to have hope too. I wanted them to have something simple, something that explained how on earth I was doing so well and being so happy, so soon after losing Ross.

The Happy Me Project was born and has been a huge success.

I am now doing The Happy Me Project Live workshops around the country and meeting my large social media following in person. I have been appearing on shows such as Lorraine Kelly, and am being asked to get involved with projects all over the place. I have been asked to speak at some incredible events and I'm being featured in magazines and books over the next year.

Success to me is waking up every day and doing what I want, it's giving back and living life on my own terms. I am already successful and being able to realise that is empowering.

That certainly does not mean I am ready to stand still. I plan to put together a self-development TV show, write a book, continue to tour the country with The Happy Me Project, adding some high-end retreats to this too, and also continue to build an incredible life for my two beautiful and brave daughters.

I truly adore working with people and helping them to unlock their potential. I am fascinated by why we do things and why some people have amazing lives, while others constantly block their own way. I am obsessed with freedom and I want everyone to have it.

I know more than ever now that life is horrifically short and I want to make a mark during my time, I want to give life a really good go. I don't feel sorry for myself; I have an incredible life and no matter how heartbreaking it has been to lose my best friend, the other half of Rolly, I know that he was happy with what he did. Ross always said to me that he had done everything he wanted to do and that he was happy. I don't think any of us can ask for more than that.

The tough parts of life is all part of the journey. I don't take myself too seriously and even though I have no problem saying I am bloody good at what I do, I also know that life is all just one big game and can flip around in a second.

This year for me is about connection, love, gratitude, and soaking up every possible opportunity that comes my way. Thank you to all of you that make this possible. To those that support me in person and online, every single message I get I appreciate.

Thank you.

Holly's top tip:

"To those that are just starting out in their entrepreneurial journey, my top tips are these:

Know what you want and the life you want but be flexible in your methods, stay loose as you never know what challenges may mean you have to change course. Don't be scared of this though; it's part of life and will make you stronger.

Create boundaries. Decide what your life rules are and be rigid on this, the boundaries stop you losing yourself along the way. You don't have to be anyone but YOU; you are enough and if you try to be someone else, you will only ever be a poor version of them.

Don't play victim. Don't feel sorry for yourself, your life is no one else's responsibility but yours.

I have had many set-backs in my working life, times when people probably thought I had lost my mind, but I always kept going. I have always kept telling my truth and known what I wanted. I still know exactly what I want. I have also allowed myself the respect to change my mind when I want to. Just because I wanted something at 20, doesn't mean I want the same thing at 33"

Holly's favourite quote:

"A man is a success if he gets up in the morning and gets to bed at night, and in between he does what he wants to do."

Bob Dylan

www.iamhollymatthews.com

TWITTER NAME:
@hollymatthews

Mehmooda Duke DL

**MANAGING DIRECTOR AND SENIOR SOLICITOR
MOOSA - DUKE SOLICITORS**

"

BE COURAGEOUS – THE FIRST STEP ON YOUR
JOURNEY IS THE HARDEST. GO FOR IT AND
DON'T LOOK BACK. BELIEVE AND IT WILL BE.

MEHMOODA DUKE DL // MOOSA – DUKE SOLICITORS

MEHMOODA DUKE DL
MOOSA - DUKE SOLICITORS

I have a dream. It's difficult to pin point when exactly my journey began, but I did have a dream for myself. That dream was to one day own my own business and to make it a success. I just didn't know what that business would be or how I would do it.

The dream is all I saw. What I didn't see were the failures along the way, challenges that I had not foreseen and moments which I had not planned for.

There have been many failures, many successes, many lessons, and many amazing surprises on this journey. I will share with you some of the most defining ones.

The Business Child

As a child, I used to make celebration cakes and sell them; I used to sell posters in school and make a small profit; I used to apply for catalogues and get the free gifts and take orders from friends at school with a small mark up.

Does anyone remember the Mike Reid breakfast show on Radio 1? I got a sought after 'Tee Hee' mug by writing in and having my article read out on the radio. I regularly had things read out on Radio 1 and got sent gifts.

So, in a small way, I was always looking for opportunities. I was wired to negotiate. I am of Indian origin - we haggle for everything (I even haggled in Harrods once and had £25 knocked off a pair of boots!).

The Teacher

Life for me began in Blackburn at a comprehensive school

where I was School Captain. I went to Cambridge University and started life as teacher of Comparative Religion. My mum had always wanted me to be a teacher, 'It is a safe career. You will have lots of holiday and it is a great career if you want to have a family.' She was right about that. I loved teaching; I was good at it; I felt comfortable. I loved the children and creating new possibilities for them every day, but I didn't feel that I had reached my own full potential in life.

I completed a year as a teacher before going to Law School in Chester.

Rude Awakenings

My biggest shock came on my first day when the class tutor asked if there was anyone in the room who had not got a training contract. Out of 200 hands only three went up; one of them was mine. My first rude awakening.

Over lunch the same day serendipity played a part – I got chatting to a mature student who asked me what kind of law I wanted to do. Now one thing I was sure of was that I wanted to do medical law (my fiancé at the time was a doctor).

Had I heard of Hempsons? Her husband was a dentist and was being defended by them. In those days (1990) there was no internet, so I went home and looked them up in the Lawyers job directory. I called them and asked if they had any training contracts. I had just missed the deadline! My second rude awakening!

However, they told me that if I got my application in that day they would consider it. I tidied up my CV, got in my car, and took it to the central post office in Liverpool. I had my CV bound and had made myself a logo. I was a perfectionist and even if it looked cheesy, it would look different from everyone else's.

I got an interview. I took a train to London and went to the law firm in Covent Garden. I wore a chocolate brown suit that my Grandma had made for me.

The experience was terrifying, I was completely out of my comfort zone. The lawyer who interviewed me was deadpan; he reacted to nothing, sat with his feet up on the desk. There was no connection. My challenge was to engage him. So, I thought on my feet and decided that I needed to make him laugh; break down the barrier. I did that and a second interview later, I had my training contract.

More Rude Awakenings

Six months before the end of my training contract I found out that Hempsons were not keeping me on after qualification. Out of three trainees, I was the failure.

But I was also very lucky because I had made friends in the legal world over the 18 months I had been there. They helped me to make connections which helped me to get another job.

I secured a job at Capsticks, the best part was that they wanted me to start immediately, so I transferred my training contract to them. Hempsons in fact head hunted me a few years later which was very flattering and for me, neutralised the original failure.

The legal dream

I have a clear memory of being a trainee at Capsticks walking past the Boss and his wife's car every morning. One day that will be me; one day I will be senior partner of a law firm. That was my personal mantra. When? How? These questions I had no answer to, yet.

The dream revised – The catalyst

Every lawyer wants to be a partner in a law firm. I was no different. The promise of partnership was the sweet carrot that kept me going. In 2000 I was headhunted by a National law firm and was promised partnership in 12–18 months. When I was then looked over for partnership, I realised that the time had come to leave. I was never going to become senior partner by climbing the corporate ladder.

The time had come to take the brave step of giving up one dream for another. I would now go and set up my law firm.

May 2003

I moved from London to Leicester in December 2002 and on the 12th of May 2003 I found myself in a one bedroom flat on

London Road with nothing more than a mobile telephone, an ancient laptop, and a £35,000 loan from my father. NTL came to install nine telephone lines because that was the smallest number that they could install on a centrex system. 'I am never going to use nine lines!', I told my brother. I only envisaged a team of four people and so it felt like a total waste.

I had no clients. No one knew who I was. I had no work, no staff, no secretary, no receptionist, nothing! I was in a flat with threadbare carpets and a desk. My filing cabinet was a tidy box – well, I had no files so why did I need a filing cabinet?

I didn't even know how to do my job properly - all I knew was how to defend doctors, not sue them!!

I did the cleaning, the photocopying, the marketing, the accounting, the books, the fee earning. I took the post to the post office, went to the bank and did the networking. I was even the receptionist! This is what happened when people rang the office:

Me (in my receptionist voice): *'Good morning Moosa-Duke Solicitors, how may I help you?'*

Caller: *'May I speak to Mrs Duke please?'*

Me (in my receptionist voice): 'Just one moment please, I will see if she is available'

Phone on hold ...

Me (in my lawyer voice): *'Hello, Mrs Duke Speaking, how may I help you?'*

...and so the journey continued until my first legal assistant joined the firm four months later.

1st Challenge – The Legal Aid Franchise

I was a defendant medical negligence lawyer - I needed to prove myself as a specialist claimant lawyer. I needed a franchise and to get on the specialist panel. With guidance from my claimant lawyer friends I got on the panel, but as for the Legal Aid franchise, I missed a crucial tender application deadline because I didn't know about it!

I was devastated as this would mean three years of being unable to do legal aid work – a crucial blow. So here I was again.

I refused to take no for an answer and appealed until I achieved the outcome I needed.

2nd Challenge – The Competition

As with any business, it is important to do your market research and find out who the competition is. My competition was five established big name law firms in Leicester.

How was little old me going to compete in this market place? The answer was simple - deliver quality and have a USP (unique selling point)! Mine was that I had a unique insight into the defendant world. I was happy to grow slowly and steadily and build a good reputation for quality work. If I did this then I knew that success would come organically.

Keep your overheads down!

One of the tips my parents gave me was to avoid spending too much unnecessary money, so when I spent £10,000 (out of my start up £35,000) on my first advert in the yellow pages, they were shocked. However, my first client from the yellow pages showed that the advert more than paid for itself.

I asked that client why they chose me; they said that if I could afford such a big advert then I must be good! An interesting lesson in psychology.

That said, the lesson in keeping your overheads down is a wise one and I have always maintained the importance of keeping an eye on this especially when starting out.

Growth and Cashflow

Medical negligence cases take about five to six years from inception to bring in any money. It was therefore critical to have some quick wins, and cashflow was crucial if the firm was to survive.

To generate cashflow, I built up a caseload of road traffic accident cases for the first few years. I knew nothing about running these cases so I took a 'crash course' (pardon the pun) and learnt quickly. I paid a referral fee and bought in some of the work. I hired two paralegals and under my supervision, we set up a personal injury department dealing exclusively with rear end shunts and passenger claims. These were guaranteed wins and unlikely to be contentious.

In the background, the clinical negligence cases continued to build and grow. I dealt with these on my own until the day that I could afford my first specialist, Krishna Kotecha.

Krishna and I met at my last firm and became friends. She was there at the lightbulb moment when I decided that Leicester might be the place to set up my firm.

I have not looked back.

The team

Although my dream was to have a business, I had no training in business and I often got things wrong. The most important thing that I have learnt is the value of my team. When I began, I was looking for 'mini mes'. That was a big mistake.

Over the years I have learnt that the best team has a diversity of skill and knowledge and a strong leader. Everyone brings different strengths to the team and makes a different and positive contribution.

Krishna was my leveller. She never believes me when I tell her that she is the best lawyer in our team.

I have learnt to surround myself with the best people available, who can deliver to the firm's high standards.

Our team has grown to 15 team members in the last 15 years.

There are external people who form part of the firm's success and are also as I see it, members of our team; they are barristers, medical experts and insurers. By way of example, we have access to the country's top neurosurgeons, top vascular surgeons, and QCs to name a few. We have worked together for 15 years and these experts are crucial to our firm's success. These specialists choose to work with us and our clients because of the relationships that we have built up.

Effective Growth and Reputation

At one stage I felt that all the firm's clients needed to see me. How wrong was I?

I learnt not to be afraid to let go.

The best piece of advice that I was given was to train my team in such a way that ensured clients received a high-quality standard of service, irrespective of whom they were dealing with at the firm.

A key factor in growing the business, and helping to ensure the consistence of quality, was having reliable processes which could be followed.

Lessons Learnt

- Be patient and don't expect a quick win; it takes time to grow a quality business and it is important to grow at a pace you can handle. It took me five years to see the kind of profit that made me feel like I had been successful.

- Aim high but be conservative in your projections – if you do this you will be able to cater for any unexpected disappointment.

- Be afraid, but use this fear to propel you instead of debilitating you. I was afraid to grow my business. I was afraid to network and get out there, but it was only when I did that the business grew. I was afraid of hiring too many members of staff and letting go. As a business owner your instinct is to stay in control, but the best thing I did was to empower people in my organisation. It makes them feel good and it frees me up to do the things that I love doing.

- Enlist the help of other professionals – they will always be willing to help. For six years I have been part of a Business group, and the professionals in it are so supportive and have been an amazing part of my journey.

- There is no such thing as a bad decision, even if it feels that way sometimes. I have had bad hires, staff who have been challenging, and even if it felt like a disaster at the time, I learnt for next time what worked and what didn't.

Surprises

In 2013 I was approached and asked to be President of Leicestershire Law Society! My first reaction was, why? And how would little me take on such an important and prestigious role? My instinct was fear, trepidation, and to say no. However, I was persuaded to step up and say yes... which eventually I did. I felt that I could not turn down such an honour, but more importantly, my reason for saying yes was that I had a responsibility as an Asian woman to be a role model and show what was achievable. I was the first Asian female to hold this position in the Law Society's 155 year history and the seventh female. I held the position for 12 months from May 2015 to May 2016.

I thought that I would do my 12 months and get back to normal life after I completed my year – but I could not have been more mistaken.

In 2016, I was approached by the University of Leicester to be a member of Council, and in 2017, I was asked by the Lord Lieutenant of Leicester to support her and become a Deputy Lieutenant for the County. I was truly humbled.

My biggest surprise came when I was nominated by business colleagues for Leicester Mercury Business Woman of the Year which I could not believe I won!

In 2017, I was also approached by Leicestershire County Cricket Club to be one of its Board Advisors and to sit on its Management Sub Committee. My cricketing friends have had to educate me in the game (I still don't know what a Googlie is) but I hope that I bring some value to the Club with my business and legal knowledge.

Key Accreditations, Appointments and Awards:

2003 - Ongoing: Awarded membership of The Law Society's Clinical Negligence Panel

2008 - Ongoing: APIL (Association of Personal Injury Lawyers) – Awarded Senior Litigator status

2011 - Ongoing: Founder member and Co-President - Fosse Business Breakfast Club

2013 - Ongoing: Executive Board founder member - Society of Clinical Injury Lawyers

2013 – Ongoing: Executive Board member of Leicestershire Law Society

2014 - Ongoing: Ranked band 1 lawyer by Chambers and Partners and described as being 'in a league of her own'

May 2015 – May 2016: President of Leicestershire Law Society

October 2016 - Ongoing: Appointed Council Member - University of Leicester

May 2017 – Ongoing: Appointed Chair of Leicestershire Law Society

June 2017 – Ongoing: Appointed to Management Sub Committee of Leicestershire County Cricket Club and Advisory Board member

June 2017 – Ongoing: Appointed Deputy Lieutenant for Leicestershire and Rutland

September 2017: Leicestershire Business Woman of the Year Award (Leicester Mercury)

Mehmooda's favourite quote:

"Some people come into our life as blessings;
some people come into our life as lessons."

Mother Theresa

Mehmooda's top tips:

1. People buy people; engage with the people around you and be the first to give and add value – the rest will come organically.

2. Be authentic in your relationships – people will see through you if you are not.

3. Give praise and thanks to your staff and all who help you.

4. Have humility and apologise when you get things wrong.

5. Don't take no for an answer and don't give up.

6. Be flexible in your approach but do not compromise your values.

7. Never underestimate the value of networking and building relationships.

8. Never undervalue your product or service – people pay for quality.

9. Stay focused – long and short term - put your phone on flight mode and set your timer!

10. Watch your overheads!

11. Growing your business –

    a. Surround yourself with a team of people who are:

       i. smarter than you

       ii. different from you

    b. Have good processes.

www.moosaduke.com

TWITTER NAME:
@MehmoodaDUke

Joanne Derviller

MANAGING DIRECTOR
IMAGINATE CREATIVE

"

DON'T EVER GIVE UP REACHING FOR THOSE
STARS AND STRIVING FOR MAGIC, NO MATTER
WHAT LIFE THROWS AT YOU; THERE IS ALWAYS
A WAY. YOU JUST HAVE TO BELIEVE WITH ALL
YOUR HEART AND IMAGINE...

...IMAGINATION DECIDES EVERYTHING.

JOANNE DERVILLER
IMAGINATE CREATIVE

What an honour to be asked to share my story with you. As probably with everyone who reads this, there are events that happen in your life that carve out your journey, some good and some bad, and I'm no different. I'm a really positive person, so my dilemma when writing this was whether I should leave out the bad stuff - or should I be transparent?

Winning the Woman Who... Achieves Awards in 2017 has had a big impact on me. It just blew me away, but more so, I found the most incredible powerhouse of support ever. Such amazing women, who are strong, yet aren't afraid to be vulnerable. Women who have shared such personal stories, that I felt the only way that I could tell you my story, was with utter honesty.

First and foremost, I'm a mommy to my beautiful children Toby and Polly and a step mommy to my precious step chidren Jay and Kyra. They are my absolute world. I have an incredible husband, Simon, who I love with all my heart. I am so blessed to have him by my side.

And I absolutely love what I do! I'm a creative designer, with a career spanning nearly 30 years. I'm the founder of four businesses, Imaginate Creative, Emaginate, Lily & Blue, and Warehouse44.

So where did it all start?

I grew up in Solihull, one of four children. My dad was a builder and my mom stayed at home to bring us all up.

To me, everything was fairly normal, until I was about 11 when things started going wrong between my parents. The worse it got, the more my dad drank, and the more he drank the worse the violent arguments got. This went on for years. Anyone who has experienced an alcoholic will know the devastating effect it has physically and emotionally on a family.

Those years growing up, were scary, painful times. But my mom is the strongest woman I know, and even though she didn't always do everything right, what she did show me through that time was sheer utter determination to get us through it and that strength has always stayed with me.

Even though things weren't great at home, at 16, with my colouring pens in hand, I headed off to college to study graphic design. I always knew I wanted to be a designer and I loved my two years at design college, learning and carving out the skills that would ultimately become my life. I would simply loose myself in typography, something that has never changed to this day.

Sadly, mainly because of what was going on at home, I didn't get the chance to go to university, something that I desperately wanted to do. So as my college course was coming to an end, I decided that I needed to find someone, anyone, who would let me come along and start work experience. So, at 17, I took out the yellow pages and started at A. I didn't get past E before someone said yes. I began work experience with a new agency of only three guys, and that's where it all began.

It was like a dream come true when at the end of the two week placement they offered me a job! I was like, YES! I finished college on the Friday and started work on the Monday and have been designing ever since.

Those first years working in a design studio were very different to how agencies look these days. There wasn't an apple device in sight, it was just you, a drawing board, and a pencil! And I loved it!

The company remained just the four of us for a couple of years, but I'm not going to lie, it wasn't easy being a young girl in the design industry 30 years ago.

Back then the industry was very male dominated, there

I AM A WOMAN WHO...

were many a time that people assumed I was the secretary, or the assistant, and that was fine, but I would take offence to the stupid sexist remarks of passing clients or suppliers. I simply couldn't understand why I was being treated different to the guys in the studio.

I am not a feminist, if anything I don't like the word, because to me gender shouldn't matter one way or another, surely! So, when it did, I used to get really annoyed about it.

But throughout it all, as the company grew, so did my bond with my two bosses, who were themselves brothers. And when my dad finally disappeared out of my life when I was 19, they really did step up to look after me, and take me under their wings, like I was their little sister.

We quickly outgrew our attic studio and moved into swanky converted barns and it was here that the company really started gathering momentum and growing, and I was instrumental in that growth. I handpicked each and every one of the creative team, and many of them I personally trained.

By the time I was 29, I was creative director running a studio of 40 designers in a company of 45, of which there were only three women, including me. We worked on some incredible, high profile projects like the 1996 Atlanta Olympics... and at the age of 30 I was finally made Partner in the business.

I loved that company, and my bosses, who by this time truly were my family. I had also met someone and had a strong relationship growing, and we had even bought our first house together! Things were rocking, I was so very happy finally.

Then something happened that was going to change everything.

It was Christmas 2001, and we were on our works Christmas party, when I was sexually assaulted by a member of my team. I am sure that there are people reading this who will understand what that feels like. I was shocked, ashamed, embarrassed, disgusted, humiliated, and most of all scared. To go through something like that changes everything. I can still feel that fear inside me today, like it happened yesterday, I don't think it ever goes away. At the time, the fear makes everything go through your head. Shall I pretend it never happened?...I've got to work with this guy!!! Should I go to the police...? Will anyone even believe me...? What will my partner say...? Will he believe me? All reason goes out the window, I was terrified.

Even though I was so scared, I knew that I couldn't keep quiet, so I made the decision to speak to my bosses. They would know what to do, they would look after me. It was probably one of the hardest, most humiliating things I have ever done. But what came next, I would never have imagined. They panicked, tried to sweep it under the carpet, they didn't know what to do or how to handle it. It was handed over to the HR director. Obviously the guy who did it denied everything - he was married with kids... it was like a living nightmare. I don't think I have ever felt so alone, ashamed, desperate, banished and frightened in my life.

But I hadn't worked so hard and dedicated so much of my life to building this business to have it all taken away from me because of someone else. So, I fought and fought. And the more I fought for my rights the worse and worse it got.

Bearing in mind that I was Creative Director, in charge of a team of designers, I was alienated from projects, I was ignored and laughed at and worse of all I was threatened. But even though I was being beaten down emotionally, I knew it was wrong, and that made me angry and I fought and fought it for a whole year.

Needless to say, I wasn't sleeping, and it wasn't until a few days later when a package arrived, I remembered buying something off the shopping channel in the middle of the night.

My life was about to change.

In the parcel, was a programme called *'Unleash the Giant Within,'* which I am sure many of you will know very well, by an amazing American motivational speaker called Tony Robbins. The programme was a 21 day course all about making change. I made it to day three! That's all it took. On day three, he talks about change, and how people think that it takes a long time to make big changes.

It doesn't. Change takes an instant.

He takes you on a journey, where he gets you to think about life - if you made that change right now, what would your life be like tomorrow, next week, next month, in six months, 12 months.... what would it look like in three years, in five years... by the time he got to five years I felt happy for the first time in a year. Then, he brings you back to the present, and asks what would life be like if you didn't make the change now, tomorrow, next week, next month, in six months, 12 months... what would it look like in three years, five years... I went from feeling happiness to utter desperation; I was in pieces again.

All of a sudden, the fear of NOT making that change became worse than the fear of taking the leap.

I went in the next day and resigned. It was the most empowering feeling in the world. I had taken back control. And Imaginate was born. I worked so hard to get it started, I literally had to start from scratch. I wanted to build a business with creativity at the heart of it. Within that first year, Imaginate grew to three, and very quickly the big projects started coming in, even clients from my last company found me and started following. I was back, and it felt amazing.

Things at home were great too. I had been with my partner now for seven years, we were engaged, and 12 months after the launch of Imaginate we discovered we were having a baby. I was over the moon. During the next nine months I worked so hard to build the business, we moved to bigger studios and took on another person.

The day finally came and I gave birth to my beautiful little girl Polly. Nothing could have been better, my world was perfect. Then another bombshell hit. When Polly was only seven weeks old her dad walked out and left us for someone else. He had been having an affair whilst I was pregnant. My world simply crumbled.

Maybe I could have handled him just leaving me, but he left the most beautiful little perfect gift I ever could have given him, and that cut very deep. I had no idea how I was going to manage. A newborn baby, a new business, a new home, and a new mortgage, with no family nearby to help. I came so close to saying this is just too difficult, I need to close the business.

But I honestly think, that the ONLY thing in life that holds us back is, *'how far you are prepared to try,'* and, *'how far you are prepared to put yourself out there.'* So, three weeks later, baby in one arm, and an apple mac in the other, I went back to work.

Over the next year we worked like crazy and the company grew from four to five. Then right in the midst of it all, running around like a crazy woman, working full time, going back and forth from the nursery with a ten month old baby, doing all the night feeds in between answering emails and doing design work.... utterly knackered...

...fate took over again!

I went on a photoshoot for a project, and fell head over heels in love with the photographer. That day I met my soulmate and future husband, Simon.

Imaginate started working on some big projects in sport, and I was asked to be a speaker at MLB's conference in Prague. At the conference, I met a man who would utterly inspire me, Ray Thomas. He was probably one of the most selfless people I have ever met, who had devoted his life to helping the children of the poor communities in Mexico where he lived. And after listening to him I just knew I had to help.

We financially supported the Mexican Yes Foundation for many years, helping to contribute to their Breakfast programme, feeding hundreds of kids a hot meal every day, and raising money for their other programs. This led us to think, what else can we do? So, we decided that each year we would do at least one pro bono project to help good causes and have worked now with some amazing people over the years, this is something that we feel very passionate about and will continue as long as we can.

The company was still growing and we brought on a team of developers, and from this came an opportunity to work alongside Worcester College. They had a need to submit all of their development records electronically but there was no software out there that did it specifically for Colleges. So we thought... okay, we'll build one!

Emaginate was born!

The software, Passport to Success has been greatly received, even on the eve of its release we were shortlisted for The Times Innovation Award. We were the first college based system ever to be recognised. We are in ten colleges nationally and are in development of Version 4 of the software.

Things at home were amazing, Simon and I married, much to the delight of our little ones, who were finally going to be 'real brothers and sisters' and 12 months later, almost to the day of our first anniversary, our little Toby was born. But about eight months later, I started to realise that something was wrong. No matter what I did, no matter how strong I tried to be, I just couldn't pull myself out of this gut retching sadness.

I ended up being diagnosed with postnatal depression. I am sure there are many people who know how that feels - even though you are surrounded by so much love and happiness, you feel like you are sitting in a little dark hole just looking out.

Needless to say, I started on medication, but me being me, I always have to focus on something positive. I used to lie in bed and look at a picture my sister had given me that had on it Toby's name, birthday, weight, etc. on it, and it made me happy. This got me thinking... seeing these words are helping me. So, what if there were more happy memories on there, places, and names of all the things that make our lives so very special.

Lily & Blue was born. We make beautiful typographical word art, filled with people's life memories. It only took me eight months to get better, but Lily & Blue still goes strong today.

Imaginate is 15 years old this year and in that time we have worked on some amazing projects including The Patrons Lunch for the Queens 90th birthday.

One project though that stands out was for a member of the Royal family in Rhyiad, Saudi Arabia. That trip was interesting! Doing a creative presentation next to a swimming pool in the Ritz

Carlton, in Rhyiad, in front of the King's Advisors, dressed in a business suit with a full abaya and hijab over the top, was slightly surreal to say the least.

But the project I am most proud of was being asked to create a one-off book for England Rugby to commemorate the 27 England rugby players who lost their lives in the first world war. The book was commissioned by Stuart Lancaster and travelled with the England team during the Rugby World Cup 2015. Prince William even read from it to the players prior to one of the games. It now lives within the Rugby World Museum, the only one in existence.

From nightclub to creative hub.

Three years ago I decided to follow another dream... to build a creative hub, in the heart of Leamington Spa, Warwickshire. For four years we searched for the perfect place until we found the old derelict Ocean Reef Nightclub. I thought, wow, this place would be amazing, but everyone was telling me not to do it, that it would be a money pit, it wouldn't work. I listened to them and walked away.

We carried on looking for 18 months and I was just about to sign the lease on a new building when I woke up at about 3am on a Sunday morning, and thought... it's got to be Ocean. I didn't know if it was still on the market, but what I did know was that if I didn't at least try, I would regret it forever.

So, I emailed the estate agent... at 3am!

Luckily it was still vacant... and derelict! It was an enormous risk, we had to pay £80,000 renovation costs upfront, which meant ploughing in all of the company's savings. But we did it... and with its stunning stained glass windows, exposed bricks and metal work, and a real urban New York loft style warehouse feel, we opened Warehouse44. We wanted to fill it with creative tenants within three years, we did it 14 months! Warehouse44 was one of the biggest risks I have ever taken in my life, but it paid off and it is now the most creative, amazing space that I could ever have wished for.

The last 30 years have had its massive ups and downs, and now is no different. Three years ago, just after we had invested everything into the Warehouse, we lost 35% of our turnover overnight, when our biggest and longest standing client merged with another global giant. With the merger came massive global restructure and the cutting of all external services, including design. I had worked with them for over 20 years, it was a huge huge blow.

Building again.

So, the last few years have been really challenging for us, trying to replace that business without having to lose people. We are not out of the woods yet, it's still really hard and the market is struggling, but we are getting there. We are made of strong stuff and most of all we believe in what we do.

I have an amazing creative team, each and everyone one of them so very talented in their own right. Each of them also embrace young talent and help drive our student placement program. We massively believe in supporting young talent, and we have a constant stream of design students with us, from school, 6th Form, College, University, and the apprentice programme.

Who knows where the next few years will take us, but one thing I do know is that I am so lucky to have had nearly 30 years doing what I love no matter what, and I will still go out there every day and try my best.

I'm still not a feminist, but what I do know is that I'm a Woman Who... a woman who is strong and determined... a woman who isn't afraid of being vulnerable... a woman who wants to make a difference in this world... and who still believes in the good of people, and will never EVER give up trying.

But most of all, I'm proud to be part of Woman Who...

Joanne's top tip:

"I made a big decision to overcome a fear and talk about things in my life, so my challenge to you... whatever decision you are putting off, big or small, whether it's calling your mum, ringing the company that you are desperate to do business with, or taking that massive life leap... just do it! Go out today and make the decision now, because I promise life gets better when you do. And remember, the only thing in life that holds us back is how far you are prepared to try."

Joanne's favourite quote:

"Surround yourself with the dreamers and doers, the rebels of the status quo, the troublemakers of the ordinary, the wonder-seekers, freedom-makers, jail-breakers, the unreasonable earth-quakers and dust-shakers, the ones who believe the impossible exists only to be attempted, the crazies & creative warriors, the ones who ask why-not instead of why, the I-can't-believe-I-bloody-did-it sort of people, and learn to dance and howl and recreate your life along with them. You may be crazy but, Dear Wolf, you're not alone."

Andrea Balt

www.imaginate.uk.com

TWITTER NAME:
@imaginateonline   @JoDerviller

Jo Stroud

FOUNDER
MANTRA JEWELLERY & FABULOUS

"

RUNNING A BUSINESS IS CHALLENGING AND
DIFFICULT, A LOT OF THE TIME. BUT THE SENSE
OF FREEDOM AND PERSONAL ACHIEVEMENT, THE
ABILITY TO BE IN CONTROL, AND THE OPPORTUNITY
TO BE CREATIVE AND ACT QUICKLY ON DECISIONS,
MORE THAN MAKE UP FOR IT. GO FOR IT!

JO STROUD
MANTRA JEWELLERY & FABULOUS

I set up my designer jewellery retail business, Fabulous, in 2005. After a career in retail and marketing, I had decided it was time to create my own business, and was determined to bring excitement and glamour to the experience of buying jewellery on the high street.

I had always loved retail, kicking off my career with Dillons' Bookstores, now part of Waterstones. Books were my first love – I studied English at university, entered all sorts of creative writing competitions, and fully expected to work in publishing as my long-term career. I also collected inspiring quotes, long before it was fashionable to do so: quotes from Oscar Wilde through to Coco Chanel peppered my walls.

But after 7 years working with books, a career move saw me join a marketing agency, working with clients such as Aston Martin and Hewlett Packard. I found I was very good at identifying a company's target customers and creating communication strategies to reach them. Seven years on, and in a senior management role at the agency, I felt it was time to set up on my own, wanting to combine my knowledge of marketing with my love of retail.

A chance visit to a jewellery shop in the Lake District, when I got married, sparked the idea. I was actually planning to visit an art gallery in Ambleside that morning, as art is a real passion of mine – but my aunt mentioned a new jewellery shop across the street. I popped in – and loved their range – but found the shopping experience difficult and frustrating. No mirrors to try things on; no information about the designers; staff who seemed unwilling to open cabinets... I became convinced that there must be a way to create shops that appealed to female customers, more in tune with the way women shop and browse, making the buying experience more relaxed and enjoyable.

On return from honeymoon, I researched the industry, and started to create the business plan for Fabulous, coming up with the name and the detail of the proposition during long walks in the Cotswolds with my husband. The two biggest growth areas in jewellery, according to MINTEL in 2004, were forecast to be female self-purchase and branded jewellery, so I created a proposition to capitalise on both.

The start-up year was tough. Back in 2005, the high street was booming: getting a unit in a shopping centre was hard, as an unknown independent, and landlords took some persuading. Securing the designers and brands that I wanted was also tough at the start when I didn't even have a shop to show them!

During my research, I talked to everyone I could find in retail, and asked complete strangers for advice, to try to get as accurate a financial forecast for the business as possible. I attended a business start-up course, and did months of financial planning on sales, margin and costs – with the information I had available.

I opened in Leamington Spa, a good town for independents, and close to where I live in Stratford-upon-Avon, in September 2005. The scariest thing about starting a retail business is signing the lease – a 10 year lease back then, with the first break clause at 5 years - and buying stock, before you have even served your first customer.

Even though the high street was strong back then, it takes a lots of effort to change people's shopping habits, encouraging them to discover a new shop and start buying from it regularly. With all my marketing knowledge, and all my detailed planning – we still finished the first Christmas £100,000 down on where I had forecast the turnover to be! I had crisis cash-flow meetings with myself every night in January, trying to figure out a way to generate revenue.

In the end, I marketed our way out – pounding pavements to hand out leaflets, driving around affluent residential areas at weekends posting leaflets through letterboxes, and creating in-store events, like 'Men's Day' with free beer!

Things went well as time progressed, and I was more sure of the proposition, so I opened a second store in 2007, in affluent Solihull, in the Touchwood Centre. This store did well, so two years later, in 2009, I opened in Milton Keynes, a city I knew well from having worked there in the past. Two years after that, we opened in Bath, in the brand new SouthGate development. Over time, we also took on a Pandora franchise store.

The business did very well, combining a mix of well-known brands alongside carefully chosen up-and-coming designers. My main objective was to seek out designers and brands before anyone else had them – often being the first in the UK to stock a brand. We were a very early stockist of Danish brand, Pandora, back in 2006; first in the UK with leading US brands like The Giving Keys and Alex and Ani; first with many European brands, introducing them to our customers.

My marketing background also helped us enormously: data capture of customers and their purchases, from day one; detailed analysis to build CRM activity; an ecommerce website from day one, integrated into our store systems; and events – such as our sell-out Summer Garden Party and our fashion shows – several times a year, to build close relationships with customers. This evolved into social media as time went on, and ensuring our in-store activity was mirrored online.

We won awards in each of our towns, over many years; gained great customer loyalty; got a 5 star rating for our website; I was twice selected as one of the 'Hot 100' in jewellery by Professional Jeweller; and reached a turnover of over £4 million. Our ten-year anniversary was marked by a sparkling Black Tie do at beautiful Mallory Court, just outside Leamington Spa.

We also tried to give back to the community throughout the years. We committed to 'Race for Life' for ten years, putting together teams of staff and customers in each town, raising thousands for charity, and always trying to make everything we did just a little bit more fabulous: we served pink bubbly at the finish line, for example, and rewarded our entrants with a charm bracelet to say thank you. We also set up a jewellery recycling initiative, 'Reloved', to raise money for Breast Cancer Now, and carried out a sponsored 30 mile walk between our stores.

Our charitable work culminated in me running the London Marathon in 2016, to raise money for Breast Cancer Now, as it was a charity we had always supported. Just weeks after the run, my mum was diagnosed with the disease, so I also ran it in 2017, this time for much more personal reasons.

Over the course of those ten years, however, several factors combined to make high street retail exceptionally challenging, and we were caught in a 'perfect storm'. The credit crunch and subsequent recession made discretionary purchases like jewellery less frequent; the growth of online purchases reduced spend on the high street; but even more importantly for us, our suppliers became our competitors.

Every large brand that we stocked now had its own ecommerce website, social media platforms and often standalone stores to reach its customers directly – therefore simply having no need for a multi-brand retailer.

Three years ago, I recognised that this was going to impact us more and more, so I decided it was time to start creating and developing our own brands of jewellery. We drew on all our years of experience of what our customers love, and the way their relationship with jewellery was changing, to develop our thinking. Now, how jewellery makes you feel, and what it means to you, is as important as what it looks like. We developed our collections with these principles in mind.

'Life's Journey' is one of our collections, which is very personal for me. It celebrates your individual journey through life, with all its twists and turns, with a philosophy of embracing the detours in life, as you never know where they might take you. The signature piece is an elliptical bangle - its shape representing life's twists and turns, and its four finishes representing the various paths you follow in life. I feel my business life has come about through a series of unplanned detours – such as walking into that jewellery shop in the Lake District all those years ago!

'Mantra', our leading brand, is meaningful jewellery, designed to inspire and uplift. Each piece symbolises a specific mantra, intended to make a positive impact on the way that you feel. The idea is to hold onto your piece of jewellery for a few moments throughout the day to bring its message to mind.

I believe that the power of words to inspire us is undeniable. An uplifting phrase, caught sight of or remembered during a busy day or tough times, is enough to remind us to stay strong, be positive, and believe in the best. It harks back to my days of collecting all those inspirational quotes, when those 'words of wisdom' seemed to me to hold valuable life lessons. I also drew heavily on inspiring words when I ran the marathon – 26 mantras; one for each mile, just to keep me going.

So, for me, Mantra beautifully combines my love of words and understanding of their power with my knowledge of jewellery. It is as if my life has come full circle, reigniting my early passion for the written word.

Mantra is now an award-winning brand, with thousands of loyal followers. It has tapped into the wellness trend that is sweeping the world, as people look for ways of gaining a moment of peace and tranquillity through their day. We have partnered with leading yoga teachers and yoga studios, for example, to create collaborative pieces.

We see Mantra mainly as an online brand, selling 70% of it online at mantrajewellery.co.uk, but we are also wholesaling it to selected retailers, so we can reach a wider audience. High street retail is still part of the mix – but the world is changing rapidly.

And in keeping with my desire to always give back, we have also set up 'Mantra Changes Lives', our charity initiative, creating uplifting necklaces to raise funds for charities such as MIND and Bullying UK. Our latest collaboration is focused on the empowerment of women, working with CARE International.

Creating and owning my own product brand – as opposed to a retail brand – has given me a freedom and opportunity that I was missing in retail. When you stock and sell other people's products, you are still constrained by their brand requirements. With our own brands, we have been able to imagine what we would ideally like to create, and then go ahead and do it!

But the switch from being a pure retailer to designer, creator and manufacturer, has been truly challenging. From finding a good manufacturing partner in Thailand, where we were determined to produce Mantra, as the quality of silver craftsmanship is so high; to creating packaging, display material and brand collateral; to the changing cashflow requirements of manufacture and wholesale, as opposed to retail, has brought a whole new learning curve for me and my team.

Over time, I have had to close retail stores and make staff redundant; I have had to renegotiate leases, play hardball, and take on tough competitors. Reinvention and moving with the times is essential in business, and this is what I have continued to do. There is never a point in business when you can stop and say, 'I've done it!', as the world around you continually changes.

I am lucky to have a great team around me, many of whom have been with me for ten years and more. We have all had a hand in evolving the business, which is one of the joys of working in an independently-owned company.

For me now, Mantra is the way forward in my business, as we move into the next stage of commercial growth. I was thrilled in December 2017 to be awarded the NatWest Everywoman 'Hera' Award, for an inspirational woman running a business for more than 10 years. Now, it is about turning Mantra into a powerful brand that can be a force for good.

I am still just as passionate about jewellery and its uniqueness: there are '5 P's of jewellery' that I believe describe its power:

"Jewellery is personal – you wear it close to you; portable – you carry it with you by wearing it; precious, in what it is made of, or what means to you; and permanent, or lasting, in a way that so

many other products or gifts simply aren't. It also acts as prompt, or reminder, of the reason you bought it, or the person who bought it for you."

And I am on a mission now, to get the message out there:

Jewellery can't change the world. But it can change the way you feel. And that can change your world.

Jo's top tip:

"Always remember that there is someone somewhere who has been in exactly the same position as you. Build a strong support network around you. Spend time with women in business who have similar values and inspire you, learn from them as they will have learned from their role models."

Jo's favourite quote:

"Change my thoughts and I change my world."

an essential reminder from the brilliant Norman Vincent Peale that we are all in control of what we think and how we react, which reminds us to think more positively.

www.mantrajewellery.co.uk

TWITTER NAME:
@MantraJewellery

Ruth Waring FCILT

MANAGING DIRECTOR AND CO-OWNER
LABYRINTH LOGISTICS CONSULTING

"

SOMETIMES YOU'LL LOSE AND SOMETIMES
YOU'LL WIN, BUT WHEN THINGS GO WRONG
AND OTHER PEOPLE UPSET YOU OR INTERFERE
WITH YOUR PLANS, REMEMBER THE ONLY
PERSON WHO CAN AFFECT YOUR EMOTIONS IS
YOU. KEEP PERSEVERING - DON'T LOSE SIGHT OF
YOUR AMBITION AND KEEP HOLDING ON TIGHT
TO YOUR DREAMS. I HOPE YOU DANCE.

RUTH WARING FCILT // LABYRINTH LOGISTICS CONSULTING

RUTH WARING FCILT
LABYRINTH LOGISTICS CONSULTING

When I was at Edinburgh University studying for a business degree, I found a Summer holiday job at Chester College. It involved looking after around 100 old age pensioners at a time, who came there for an excursion-based holiday: I met them off the train, organised trips for them in the daytime, their entertainment at night, sorted out all their issues and problems – everything!

It was a huge responsibility for a girl straight from college with no experience of managing anything except herself. And I just thrived on the whole process – planning schedules, booking venues and transport, interacting with pensioners, venue managers, and coach drivers, keeping things running smoothly, and dealing with the inevitable issues and disasters.

I learned so much about myself – I realised I'm really good at organisation and schedules, that I can be very resourceful and self-reliant, and I'm good in a crisis. And I loved being at the centre of a complex set of interlocking activities; interacting with all the people and processes needed to keep everything running and everyone feeling positive, staying on track, and having a good time.

This was the catalyst that led to me choosing a career in logistics where I could use these traits and recreate the buzz of being at the centre of a big enterprise.

I've worked in logistics for 28 years now - I joined the NFC (now DHL) on graduation in 1989, working for Exel Logistics on the Marks and Spencer contract. I spent a very tough and lonely year in France implementing the M&S IT system to the Parisian warehouse before returning to the UK to work as a Traffic Manager for Exel in Coventry in 1991, rotating early/late/night shifts in charge of up to 50 LGV 1 drivers. Sometimes working the nightshift at the Coventry depot, I would be the only woman in the building. I put up with some difficult stuff so I would not be perceived as a troublemaker - I was bombarded with stories by male colleagues, often citing events from years previously, about women who didn't cut the mustard, failed to drive lorries and even the old chestnut, 'went off and had babies.'

It was a pretty tough introduction to working life and being a young woman in that environment I felt that my natural personality - bubbly, chatty, interested in people as well as tasks - was too young and 'girly' and didn't fit in. I had one other female colleague in a similar role and we helped each other a lot – looking out for each other, supporting each other when the other was not around, and swapping notes and advice. It helped me understand the power of mutual support networks.

I loved logistics and wanted to stay with it; I decided I would have to toughen up considerably to survive; put the female part of my personality away to an extent; tone my personality down; dress more conservatively and try to fit in more if I was going to realise my ambition. Of course, I needed to grow up and into my adult professional self but there was the added pressure of being in such a male dominated, traditional industry and having to prove that as a woman I was up to the job. I made the decision to change and my career progressed well, but I always felt that there was some aspect of my character I was suppressing. Finding out what life is like at the sharp end of a male-dominated industry, I felt that I wanted to do something to make things better for myself and others.

It was at this point that the idea to launch a support network for women in logistics came to me, although it took some years still before I could see a way to make it happen. I knew that women made great logisticians and I wanted to re-brand women to the logistics industry, showing them to be capable multi-taskers, often with good language skills, who can work with drivers and customers in a different but equally effective way. Yes, we do have babies – I had two - but we will come back as strong team members if the logistics industry looks after us and shows they want us back.

My career continued to progress and I gained valuable experience across the industry. In 1993 I moved to Gefco UK, the logistics arm of Peugeot/Citroen; my role was one of project manager, overseeing the move in-house of a £6m parts distribution contract to garages across the country. This involved setting up a network of six depots and over 100 vehicles across the country, TUPE transfers and vehicle/O Licence acquisition.

I then moved across to work on European Roadfreight, frequently travelling in Europe and speaking French again. Finally, I was promoted to Midlands Regional Manager, with responsibility for four depots and keeping the 'Just in Time' deliveries to the production line at Peugeot Ryton on schedule. I was responsible for over £20m turnover per annum including an import/export hub and a UK pallet hub and managing 103 members of staff (with 11 direct reports) plus 30 drivers.

In 2000 I left Gefco to join Pearson Education, then the world's largest academic publisher, as their Transport Logistics Manager. Here I controlled £2.5m Transport spend for UK domestic and export freight, in charge of the distribution over 50m books per annum.

Despite spending years in multinationals learning the industry it was always my ambition to be self-employed and to run my own business – I wanted to be responsible for my own destiny and to have the chance to use my energy and skill to build a business based on my own vision.

Growing up, both my parents were self-employed so I knew a lot about the pros and cons of working for myself. I knew that taking the step was important to me, but I had enough insight to see that aspects of the change would be tough for me and I decided to work with a life coach to help me deal with this. I am great believer in getting a coach to help you when you are making a big change but if it is not possible, read Fiona Harrold's book, Be Your Own Life Coach. Being your own boss means having to put yourself out there and experience disappointments and rejection personally without the cover of a large organisation. The coach and I worked together on building a strong sense of my own inner core of belief in my personal ability and strengths and my business goals and objectives. We worked on how I could go out and sell my services and not take failure or rejection personally; I'm thankful I invested the time and effort it involved. It was also vital to ensure that my husband Graham was happy and on board with all my plans, as I was very aware that my confidence and total faith in my plans might not be universal. He got on board with the scheme and we were off.

In January 2002 I achieved my ambition to become a self-employed logistics consultant, and then in 2003 went on to become MD of Labyrinth Logistics Consulting; a privately-owned supply chain and logistics consultancy based in Leamington Spa. Labyrinth has evolved to focus, very successfully, on two core offerings: compliance services for the UK transport industry, and logistics strategy and procurement support, mainly for companies outsourcing their logistics operations. In 2008 my business partner Jo Godsmark joined me and we have gone from strength to strength, working brilliantly together as a team. Customers range from blue chip household names to small hauliers.

An important aspect of how I have enriched this second, self-employed part of my professional life and built and developed my business, Labyrinth Logistics, is the emphasis I put on communicating and networking. I have always enjoyed networking and had a natural flair for it – I am well known in the industry for my ability to work a room, 'Ruth knows everyone!'. I believe every conference, seminar, exhibition, or meeting is a great chance to reach out to people and expand my network and I love using social media and blogging. Although much of this comes naturally to me I have also worked on my technique to get the best out of these opportunities – in fact I made a hugely successful contribution to the FIATA air freight world congress opening ceremony in Dublin in October 2016 introducing around 1,000 people to my top networking tips. These centre around the following key principles:

- Be focused on what you are looking to achieve from specific networking events; ask for the list of attendees in advance if this is available: the organisers can only say no!

- Offer to help the other person with contacts and introductions before asking for help for your business.

- Ask for contacts in a specific company or geographical area: the chances are they won't know anyone, but they will start to think laterally about contacts they might have in similar businesses.

- Paint a verbal picture of what you do which a 12-year-old could understand: I say, 'We help people who have lorries going in and out of the gate.'

- Avoid industry jargon and if someone helpfully asks, 'What types of clients could I help introduce you to?' do not say, 'We are looking for any businesses really.' Even if you do work for all types of clients say, 'We specialise in helping smaller retailers get their voice heard – do you know anyone who runs a shop?' for example, rather than something wishy-washy. This will unlock their thinking and could end up with a lead for you.

I engage with people at all levels of my industry and in my local business community, particularly women. Maybe because I felt isolated at times in my early career and found the support of others so important, I always want to reach out to build a community of people who are mutually supportive and working to improve things. I take up every opportunity I can to get involved with industry forums and initiatives, running seminars, judging awards, and speaking at conferences. This has been personally rewarding for me in the relationships and friendships I have developed and has opened up many professional opportunities and recognition.

- In 2010 I became a Fellow of the Chartered Institute of Logistics and Transport (UK).

- In 2012 I was proud to be involved in the training of hauliers on managing delivery schedules during the Olympic and Paralympics in support of the London Olympics.

- In 2013 I was selected as a Board member of the Chartered Institute of Logistics and given a role specifically created for me to represent the interests of women in the sector – the first time such an appointment had been made.

- I have contributed to the Department of Transport Working Committee which is tackling HGV driver shortage in the UK.

- In 2013 I won the FTA everywoman in Transport 'Industry Champion Award'.

- I was awarded the 2016 Leamington Business Person of the Year.

- I was 'Runner Up' in the Nat West Entrepreneur of the Year Innovation category (Midlands).

- In 2017 I was named for the third time on the LOGISTICS 100 list of the most influential players in the Logistics industry chosen annually by SHD Logistics Group.

- In 2017 I won the Pride of Warwickshire Business Person of the year award.

In 2006 more concrete plans for the Women in Logistics (WiL) group idea began to crystallise in my mind and, via a consultancy project, I pulled together a list of women in the industry who might be interested in getting a group off the ground – the challenge then became how to fund the launch. By 2008 LinkedIn had reached its tipping point and I spoke to the WiL group in the USA, they advised setting up the group as free to join and based on sponsorship in kind. This concept, coupled with the free LinkedIn group potential, was a lightbulb moment. It was both terrifying and brilliant. It risked alienating key players in the industry, where I was and am still involved on a day-to-day basis for consultancy work, but I felt that the pieces had fallen into place and that the impetus was there to start something that could change things for the better.

I contacted Clare Bottle whom I had met through the original project I had run; I knew she was very keen to get a group off the ground. A plan was hatched in Sept 2008 using the LinkedIn forum to gather potential members and tell them about the Women in Logistics UK (WiL UK) group. By January 2009, 40 members had joined and 20 turned up for the face-to-face planning meeting. The basic principles of WiL were adopted – men were invited to join, it would be free to attend with most events free of charge, there would be a free mentoring programme and the whole thing would be run by a steering team – volunteers put their hands up and the group was off the ground. Since then the group has grown to over 3,600 members, including 600 men. It hosts educational, industry and networking events, sets up mentoring relationships offering support and advice - sometimes simply by connecting people with friendly faces. It has widespread support from senior industry figures and industry bodies and has become the 'go-to' group when the industry needs input on diversifying and expanding the workforce. It runs an annual charity ball and has raised over £45K in the last five years for its chosen charity Transaid, and in that time my business partner Jo Godsmark has also become Transaid's Chair of the Board of Trustees. WiL UK is in the process now of becoming part if the Chartered Institute of Logistics and Transport (UK) - we have reached the point where we need to join forces to achieve significant further progress.

During this time Labyrinth Logistics' consultancy service was getting busier and busier. I was doing a lot of travelling and was finding this more and more difficult. I wanted to reduce my motorway mileage and exposure to road risk, and to do something about my concern that I was uncovering the same old issues and lack of consistent transport compliance management in the companies I worked with. I felt there was an opportunity to make some changes that would improve my working life and also the working practices of the industry - the old approach of paper-based compliance auditing could be done in an elegant and massively more efficient manner. I became convinced that the future of compliance was in cloud-based services rather than physical audits.

My business partner Jo Godsmark and I took the major step of diversifying Labyrinth's consultancy business, by developing and launching an online application for managing logistics compliance which we named SilkThread* in a reference to the Greek myth in which Ariadne gives Theseus a silk thread which he can use to find his way out of the labyrinth: so, the product is a navigational aid in a complex environment.

Launching a software application has changed the professional lives of Jo and I completely. We have both gone from being hands-on consultants to tech entrepreneurs and business leaders; we work with software developers and website designers, we have invested in a CRM system, we employ marketing and telemarketing agencies, exhibit at trade exhibitions, and have worked with Government departments, all to drive this venture forward. We still do the consultancy too.

It's no small task to introduce a completely new way of working to an industry and we have had a few false starts and difficulties, but SilkThread® has had amazing success to date: growing sales, positive customer feedback, winning multiple industry awards, attracting investment, and gaining grants for further development and launching new modules.

In 2016:

- Labyrinth won a T-TRIG (Transport Innovation) grant with the DfT,
- Labyrinth was awarded the CILT award for Excellence in Information management for SilkThread®.

In 2017:

- We won a growth grant from Warwickshire County Council,
- We successfully attracted three investors to the business,
- We gained certification to ISO 9001:2015,
- Labyrinth won the Leamington Business Awards Innovation of the Year Award,
- Labyrinth's client Secured Mail won the 2017 SHD Logistics Technology Innovation award for its use of SilkThread® in partnership with Labyrinth Logistics,
- Labyrinth was the winner in the Business Innovation category and Overall Winner in SME Coventry and Warwickshire Business Awards.

Looking back, I'm overwhelmed to see the positive changes to the logistics industry that I have been involved with and the exciting potential for more diversity in the workforce and better use of technology in logistics, which are central to my own interests and career path.

The logistics landscape is changing at a fast pace with continued globalisation of businesses and supply chains, technology and automation developments, environmental concerns, and workforce shortages and this means the industry has to evolve and change to meet the needs of the 21st century. I'm still excited at the prospect of creating a lasting legacy from Labyrinth and SilkThread®, and seeing what the WiL UK network can go on to achieve in developing and opening up opportunities for women working more closely in partnership with the whole of the profession. And I can't wait to see what other opportunities and challenges the future might hold for me. I am hoping to create a world where my two sons, Matthew and Johnny, will have a positive career experience if they choose to enter the logistics profession and one where it is perfectly normal, and indeed celebrated, to see a woman doing well.

I'll keep on looking for opportunities to create positive change for myself and the industry, making connections with people and organisations and working on creating the plans and momentum that can make good things happen.

Ruth's top tip:

"My top tip would be that however bad
a situation is – even if you decide to walk away -
always try to leave things on a positive note. Don't
burn any bridges, remember it's a small world and
staying on good terms could bring unexpected
benefits to you in the future."

Ruth's favourite quote:

"You playing small doesn't serve the world.
There's nothing enlightening about shrinking so
others won't feel insecure around you. As you let
your own light shine, you indirectly give others
permission to do the same."

Marianne Williamson

www.labyrinthsolutions.co.uk

TWITTER NAME:
@RuthWaring

Karen Green

MENTOR, AUTHOR AND SPEAKER
FOOD MENTOR

"

ENJOY THE JOURNEY!! LIFE IS SHORT –
I HAVE HAD SOME FANTASTIC LIFE
EXPERIENCES AND SOME REAL DISASTERS
BUT FOR THE MOST PART, I AM ENJOYING
THE JOURNEY AND YOU SHOULD TOO –
DON'T STAY STUCK IN A RUT THAT YOU
ARE NOT HAPPY WITH – PLEASE LIVE
YOUR EXTRAORDINARY LIFE!

KAREN GREEN
FOOD MENTOR

Let me introduce myself; I am Karen Green, a woman who... is a business mentor, successful Amazon best-selling author, and speaker dedicated to ensuring food SMEs achieve profitable growth, whilst their owners and leaders protect their well-being and don't get stressed out by the whole process.

I have been in the UK retail industry pretty much all my working life, from a Saturday girl in a department store, to buying at Tesco and Boots, to commercial director for various food manufacturers.

I have always had a love of food and new product development – right back from when I used to design elaborate mud pies in the garden!

So this is my business story. Giving you the heads up on what has shaped my thinking and developed my business philosophies, and candidly telling you what went wrong and how I dealt with it – learning how to pick myself up, dust myself off and start all over again!!

Baby steps into food and retail

I was born into retail. My father was the manager of a department store in Newbury and my mum worked on the make-up counter until she got married, when traditionally women stopped work – how things have changed... for the better!

I started work as a Saturday girl learning the mantra, 'retail is detail', folding jumpers with precision and ensuring the hangers all faced the same way. I learnt how to talk to customers, find out and fulfil their needs, and handle their complaints. All skills that have held me in good stead during my career! However, I found the work repetitive and boring doing the same thing every day and so instead of following my father into store based retail, I set off to university to study business studies in Manchester – a big multicultural city compared with provincial Newbury. I encountered the most amazing new foods – there was an Algerian takeaway that sold kebabs, and the most fabulous Greek restaurant that made a Stifado that has stayed with me forever!

I had always been very successful academically and going to university gave me my first real encounter with failure and the need to rethink my path. By the end of the first year, I discovered that my grades on the Maths part of my joint honours degree (with Management Science) were not good enough and I could have ended up with a 3rd class degree, which was not really in line with my plans. So, I took the decision to drop Maths and focus on my real love which was marketing and psychology (the only subject I got firsts in!) – this proved to be a good decision and I got a 2:1 degree. Note to self: focus on what you are good at rather than slaving over stuff that you are just not going to master!

Working with the big boys

I joined Tesco as a marketing graduate trainee working in Terry Leahy's team (who would go on to run the company, of course!). My first boss, Mike Coupe (currently CEO of Sainsbury's) had just arrived from Unilever as a fresh-faced marketer and we worked together on eggs, fish, and poultry. It was an interesting couple of years and I had many great experiences. I took my first flight – to visit a fish factory and negotiate my first supplier deal – yes, the shiny-faced assistant buyer of 21 who thought she knew everything coming to tell the supplier who had been smoking fish for many years, what to do!! I spent my 21st birthday in Malton Bacon Factory at my first abattoir trying not to cry as the pigs were being slaughtered... happy memories!! I think it taught me how to put on a confident face and keep going, even when inside you are just dying! A useful skill for later life!

I decided that Tesco was not for me as they wanted to take me down a buying career path and I wanted to do 'proper' brand marketing so I left after two years and went to start a career with Boots that lasted 14 years. I began as assistant brand manager and thought I had died and gone to heaven! I left behind the 4am starts on Grimsby Fish Market and moved to work with advertising and PR agencies who took me to long lunches in very expensive restaurants. Money was no object in the late Eighties and it was a lot of fun. I learnt a lot about brand marketing but I missed the breadth of retail, so I returned to my roots and crossed back to Boots the Chemist.

I spent many happy years as a food buyer – mostly buying vitamins where my passion for nutrition and healthy eating began. I learnt lots of negotiation techniques which would not be considered acceptable now in the face of GSCOPs (Grocery Suppliers Code of Practice) and I did well, driving margins up and getting substantial contributions to marketing and promotional funds and several promotions up the corporate ladder. My boss said I was the best buyer she had ever had – and we did exceptionally well. She became my first real mentor and I learnt many things from her about being tough, creative, and building the right team around me. She led me from buying to selling, and together, we moved to Boots contract manufacturing where I had my first foray into selling toiletries to Safeway. I was also given one the best jobs of my career as Head of New Product Development (NPD) for dental. I learnt a lot in those roles about people management (especially of people who were not of my background – scientists and technologists), product development strategy, and retailer strategy.

Moving into food – real food that is!!

However, I have to admit that the corporate, risk adverse culture of Boots was a challenge for me to cope with. I never felt I fitted in and was always trying to adapt my personality to meet their requirements. One of the things I learnt is that to be the best, you have to be the whole person and so when a voluntary redundancy opportunity came up, I grabbed it with both hands. My husband thought I was mad – leaving a secure job with a good pension for nothing. I had no job to go to but with a pot of cash, I decided it would be just fine and with rash enthusiasm and two young children, I jumped ship. Part of the redundancy deal was an outplacement package which was absolutely fantastic – I learnt so much about how to network, self-presentation, and personal marketing skills that have held me in good stead throughout my life.

So I began my commercial life, first in fizzy pop, and then moving finally into real food – ready meals, salads, Christmas puddings and turkeys. My emphasis was largely on own label which allowed me to grow my love of new product development and, occasionally, to indulge my love of food, being paid to go to Michelin-starred restaurants! I continued to develop my love of NPD and creating profitable sales growth through strong category strategies. I also learnt a lot about dealing with the retailers at the height of their pre GSCOPs tough tactics phase – I realised that whilst I had been a great negotiator at Boots, these guys had been trained in a whole different set of skills...

Being called for meetings at 4pm on a Friday and then the buyer walking out after five minutes... the buyer threatening to complain to my boss and have me sacked... spending three months trying to recoup thousands and thousands of pounds which a retailer clearly owed us but not realising they were withholding the money deliberately.

These were tough times for me to learn how to deal with these challenges. My lowest point came when I joined a frozen food company who had just pulled themselves out of administration and rebuilt their factory after a fire and were ready to get back on their feet. But sadly, the script for failure had already been written even before I joined. They had a retailer supply agreement that made only 4% gross margin and similar contract manufacturing deal with a major brand. There was a clause in the contract packing deal that said inflation could be passed on only after 6 months' notice. Then disaster struck with massive inflation in their two key raw materials, and those slender margins turned into significant loss. Try as I might to renegotiate the contracts, I failed and the business went into administration leaving several hundred people out of work and I personally lost a lot of money from unpaid fees! I felt very personally responsible that I had not been able to help that company and whilst there were other issues as well, it taught me two lessons that are now the backbone of my mentoring: make sure you make a decent profit from day one, and don't be afraid to walk away from a business that doesn't serve you.

The light bulb moment!!

Those dealings with the retailers were immensely difficult and stressful times and I was ready to throw in the towel, but by now I was a single mother with two young children to support, so I had to keep going and work in the industry I loved, albeit in a difficult situation. I have always been keen on training and personal development and was lucky enough to be funded by an employer to do a negotiation course run by Sentinel Management. They use ex-buyers from the UK grocery retailer base, and all the things I suspected about how the buyers used psychological techniques to constantly undermine the account manager were true, but for me that was the 'light bulb' moment that people talk about. I learnt techniques on that course that I still use today and teach to my clients. I understood how to build a selling proposition, how to deal with negotiation tactics, and much more.

And I took that learning to my final full-time role as commercial director at an own-label sushi manufacturer – ichiban UK. We supplied sushi to Tesco and Boots and also launched a brand. My career had come full circle back with the two retailers I started with. I had a great deal of success there, pushing through inflationary increases, developing some amazing products, and significantly growing the category. We launched the Yumie sushi brand that sold over £500k sales in six months, gaining strong listings. The business went from loss to £1.4m profit in two years and I also built a strong and powerful team, which was a fabulous experience and I still miss them.

Creating The Food Mentor

About a year before I left ichiban, I decided I wanted to move to France where I owned an apartment and experience a different way of life. A full time role was not possible and so I decided to create a business that was more location independent whereby I could help food companies to create profitable growth, but through mostly Skype mentoring rather than hands on, face to face work. I already had three years of mentoring experience through my volunteer work with the Princes Trust, so felt I was well able to make the transition.

So in October 2016, I sold my house, packed up my belongings (well to be honest, I sold most of them as moving from a four bed house to a one bed apartment you don't need quite the same amount of stuff!!) and moved to sunny Antibes where I now live part of the time. I come back to the UK once a month where I meet clients, do speaking gigs, and spend time with my family.

I have been lucky to have a breadth of clients from large businesses such as running market research in Prague, with no translator, about bagged salads (no, I don't speak Czech), to smaller businesses who are literally starting up, writing their first business plan and route to market. I do some guest lecturing at Nottingham Trent University and give back through my volunteer work for Virgin Start up. I am also a Judge at the Quality Food Awards and Great Taste which are the best two days of the year, seeing all these inspirational food products – although it can be difficult making decisions about whose are the best!!

To help market my business and also support clients who maybe don't have the funds to take on a mentor, I have written my first book, Recipe for Success: the Ingredients of a Profitable Food Business. It was the highlight of 2017 for me and on launch date reached Number two in the Amazon best sellers list for food books. I was truly humbled and grateful to all the people who helped me to write the book and sped to me to the top.

I love the variety of what I do and the opportunity to make a difference; to enable people to take charge of their food business and to find a love for what they do.

Summary

So, what have I learnt from my business journey? I think there are three common themes running throughout that underpin the business philosophy I now use to work with my clients:

Never stop learning – from university, to the myriad of courses that Boots sent me on, to the courses I have also produced – I have never stopped learning. I have a massive collection of business books that have helped me such as, Indestructible Self Belief by Fiona Harrold (which I recommend a lot), Tim Ferris's The 4-Hour Work Week (and almost the day after I read it, I took on two new clients and worked 60 hour weeks for three months), and many, many titles on business planning, making a profit etc. Writing my book, talks, and lectures, help me to keep on learning so I can pass on the newest thinking to my clients. I attend webinars on social media, including how to write a best-selling book and how to be happy!! Some have been mediocre, some great, but every time, I get one or two nuggets that help me grow and develop as a person

Don't be afraid to be wrong (and change direction) – Throughout my career, I have taken some twists and turns that have left me in difficult situations. Not long after leaving Boots, I decided to change career direction and retrain as a personal trainer – I loved the training, enjoyed working with clients to help them grow but realised that I would not make enough money that way so I bought a gym (as you do!). I ran it alongside doing my food sales roles for three years where my commission paid to keep my expensive hobby alive. In 2009 during the recession, I lost a food consulting client, 30% of our gym members cancelled to save money, and I was forced to declare myself bankrupt. However, I picked myself up, dusted myself off and kept on going. I was wrong to buy the gym but it taught me a lot about running a small business, local marketing, and generating profitable sales (or not!)

Focus on what you are passionate about – I love helping people to achieve their best and the best way I know to do that is through sharing my knowledge, skills and experience to get them to achieve their goals.

I have always loved food and retail from childhood and I am still passionate about it. My daughter and I love travelling and we go to retailers all over the world to look at their food products – trying them, seeing how they are packaged and just experiencing how the world eats. I love everything about it.

A long time ago, I remember getting very excited whilst out with my husband saying – 'oh my goodness, look WH Smith have changed their carrier bags' – he said something like 'get a life' – but really that IS my life! Every day seeing new products, new routes to market – food retail is constantly evolving and I am eternally grateful to be part of that.

Karen's top tip:

"Focus works! Most entrepreneurs have a myriad of ideas and thoughts about what they want to do with their business – be razor sharp in your business clarity on what you want to achieve and keep on the path. Work with mentors and people who may have the skills you are lacking but remember you are the leader of your business, so stay focused on the end goal – so much time can be wasted going down blind alleys or creating a proposition that is too wide to enable successful marketing, consumer understanding, and is too costly."

Karen's favourite quote:

"Alice: *Would you tell me, please, which way I ought to go from here?* The Cheshire Cat: *That depends a good deal on where you want to get to.*

Alice: *I don't much care where.* The Cheshire Cat: *Then it doesn't much matter which way you go.*

Alice: *...So long as I get somewhere.* The Cheshire Cat: *Oh, you're sure to do that, if only you walk long enough."*

Lewis Carroll, Alice in Wonderland

www.foodmentor.co.uk
TWITTER NAME: @KG_foodmentor

Louise Stewart

HEAD OF COMMUNICATIONS
FEDERATION OF SMALL BUSINESSES

"

MY ADVICE IS TO NOT LET ANYONE PUT
BARRIERS IN YOUR WAY – FOR ME IF SOMEONE
SAYS I CAN'T DO SOMETHING IT MAKES
ME MORE DETERMINED TO DO IT. AND DO
REMEMBER, AS I FOUND OUT WHEN I WAS
DIAGNOSED, LIFE CAN BE SHORT – SO MAKE
THE MOST OF EVERY DAY AND SEIZE EVERY
OPPORTUNITY.

LOUISE STEWART // FEDERATION OF SMALL BUSINESSES

LOUISE STEWART
FEDERATION OF SMALL BUSINESSES

Until 2015 I was a BBC TV and radio journalist – I was a political correspondent who'd covered several General Elections, the Scottish Referendum, interviewed Prime Ministers including Tony Blair, Gordon Brown and David Cameron for national news, including News at Ten, Breakfast, Radio 4 Today and 5 Live, as well as regional TV and radio.

I suppose I was lucky as I'd always known I wanted to be a TV journalist, I grew up wanting to be a war correspondent – admiring Kate Adie as she reported on the first Gulf War.

So, when I graduated I knew what I wanted to do but getting into it was trickier. I applied – along with 10,000 other hopefuls – for one of ten places on the BBC's graduate trainee scheme. Perhaps not surprisingly I didn't get a place.

One thing I realised when I went to the assessment day was that coming from a small town in the north of Scotland and having attended a local comprehensive school I was very much in the minority. I was one of the only candidates who hadn't attended private school and who hadn't then gone on to study at Oxford or Cambridge. Suddenly, I felt my degree from Aberdeen University and post-graduate from Glasgow wasn't going to cut the mustard.

It was a bit of a wake-up call not getting on the scheme but - and maybe this was down to the ignorance of youth - I wasn't deterred from pursuing my chosen career.

So I moved to London and started freelancing at ITN – right at the bottom as a script runner – delivering Trevor McDonald's scripts for the evening news programme.

It obviously wasn't a long-term career prospect but it got my foot in the door in the heart of London.

I was only earning pin money though and if it wasn't for the kindness of a successful aunt who let me stay for free I wouldn't have been able to stay in London.

I knew I had to find a proper job and as I was sending out my CV far and wide, I actually received a call from the head of BBC North West. They said the trainee they had picked had dropped out and did I want to take their place?

Obviously, I was delighted – though a little surprised as the feedback had been that I wasn't Scottish enough for the position I had originally applied for at BBC Scotland (despite being born and raised there). However, I was soon off to Manchester where I'd never been before!

I joined my fellow trainees for the course in Bristol – they were as I'd found at the assessment day; mostly ex public school pupils and Oxbridge graduates. The BBC talks a great deal about diversity at the moment but let me tell you, that intake definitely didn't feel very diverse! And as you will have seen by recent media coverage things tend to change very slowly in an organisation the size of the BBC.

Don't get me wrong, I loved my time at the BBC and had some incredible experiences – reporting in Brussels, Strasbourg, New York, etc. but I still find it hard to believe that when I left the BBC just over a year ago, I was still the only female political editor in all 15 of the BBC's nations and regions.

After I had queued for hours to interview David Cameron as PM, the first thing he said to me was 'nice shoes'. Many said I should have felt insulted, but I think after 14 men in suits he was just surprised to see me.

The issue of equal pay has dominated the news agenda for months and it was an issue I raised whilst at the BBC. I could see it wasn't going to change in my time and that was one of the reasons I decided to move on – to be appreciated for the skills I have and not made to feel I wasn't as deserving as my male colleagues.

Many people were surprised when I gave up a 20 year career at the BBC to join the FSB as head of media, but the thing is for women in TV, apart from the very few at the top, it is still a pretty perilous career. I felt as a woman in her early forties I really had hit a ceiling.

So, when the opportunity came to join the Federation of Small Businesses as Head of Media I decided to go for it. It was a new challenge and a new career.

I suppose when I joined I had this image of business being very male dominated and it being hard to break through. I think it can still be the case but at the FSB the Chief Operating Officer is a woman, so are several of the senior management team – including myself – and women are working for the organisation at all levels making a huge contribution right across the country.

It also feels much more of a meritocracy than the media. No one has asked me what school or university I attended, instead they judge me on my ability to deliver.

No one was more surprised than me when just after my three month probationary period, I was called in by the Chief Operating Officer – I was rather anxious they weren't happy with my performance – but instead she said they wanted to promote me to overall Head of Communications.

I think that felt like vindication for me for my decision to leave the BBC. I had chosen a new career and proved that I could make a success of it.

But just as I was making plans for my new role, I was in for another shock. A month after being promoted and just four months after leaving the BBC I was diagnosed with breast cancer.

There were none of the usual signs – no lump for example, but I had a pain in my left side and felt really exhausted so I went to the GP. They said it was very unlikely to be anything serious but they'd send me for tests.

Within a week I had been diagnosed with a tumour in my left breast and the following week, on my birthday, they called to say they'd found two more tumours – a second in the left side and one in the right.

I'm not sure anything can really prepare you for that moment. Having breast cancer in one side seemed very unlucky – having it in both seemed really bloody unfair! In fact only around 3-5% of women have it in both sides at the same time!

After the initial shock, I was quickly sucked into the system of hospital appointments, tests and waiting for results.

It all seemed so alien and a million miles away from my new job in London.

One of my first thoughts was how would I cope with my job? Obviously the BBC is a huge organisation with a reputation for looking after staff, but I wasn't there anymore.

I needn't have worried – the FSB have been fantastically supportive financially, and ensured me not to worry about work, just to worry about getting better.

After my treatment I felt that I wanted something good to come out of an awful diagnosis, so at the start of this year, with my employer's support, I helped launch Cancer Research UK's campaign to raise awareness of the importance of early diagnosis.

In total I was off work for five months – so by the time I returned to my role I had been off for longer than I'd actually been there.

But I am now back at work full time in a hugely busy role – if you'd told me that would be the case when I was first diagnosed I wouldn't have thought it would be possible. In March this year I was named one of the 100 most influential people in PR by PR Week, which felt like a great accolade, particularly after such a long period off work.

Sometimes, it feels like that period of my life happened to someone else. But I do always remember what my surgeon said to me when I saw her for my one-year check-up when she told me I was in remission. She said, 'Louise, you've been given a second chance at life now go and live it.' And that's what I'm determined to do.

Louise's top tip:

"I believe you have to trust your instincts and don't let the doubters put you off from achieving your ambitions. I left a very secure job with a national broadcaster to start a new career – something many people thought I was mad to do – but I genuinely have no regrets."

Louise's favourite quote:

My favourite quote is by Madeleine Albright, who was the first woman to become Secretary of State for America. She said:

"There is a special place in hell for women who don't help other women."

I truly believe that and have made it my mission to mentor and support younger women coming through behind me.

www.fsb.org.uk

TWITTER NAME:
@FSBLouiseS

Jenny Hudson

FORMER MANAGING DIRECTOR
SWEET AS CAKES

"

UNWAVERING DETERMINATION, GRIT,
FOCUS, HARD WORK, AND BELIEF WILL
GET YOU ANYWHERE.

JENNY HUDSON
SWEET AS CAKES

Ifelt stupid all the way through school. I have dyslexia and remember from my first day in reception getting a 'fuzzy brain' whenever I was asked to sit down, write, spell, or add up. This lead to me becoming a very shy girl. I isolated myself; after all, if I kept myself to myself I couldn't feel stupid. One day in secondary school I remember putting my hand up to answer a question in class, 'What is the Queen's surname?' I knew this. I proudly put my hand up. 'Royal!' I said out loud. The whole class (including the teacher) broke into hysterics. Tears stung my eyes. I never put my hand up again.

I left school with maybe four GCSEs, one being Catering which I loved. It reminded me of the lovely times I spent with my Nana making soda bread, pastry, and Irish stew. I decided to look at catering college as there was a good one locally. My parents tried everything to talk me out of it, they took me to see local chefs who would say, 'the kitchen is no place for a girl' and, 'the hours are horrible and you won't get paid much', but I was already hooked. Days after starting at catering college I knew this was the career for me. FINALLY, I was good at something! I'd stay in after classes, cooking at every opportunity and watching students in the years above me for inspiration.

After three years I was offered work experience at Claridge's in Mayfair. What an amazing experience! We were cooking fantastic food for superstars and royalty daily. I loved every second and had a great mentor in chocolate expert Claire Clarke. After my six weeks work experience I was offered a job and jumped at the chance. I enjoyed a few years hard graft in London, including stints at a bakery and fine dining for a corporate wealth management bank. I travelled around Australia for six months working in various cafes and cake shops - I'd never seen the kind of cakes that they had there before. Stunning! I knew there and then that I would combine my classical pastry chef training with new and modern ideas I had picked up travelling.

I returned to my home in Warwickshire and worked for a start-up mail order cake company in the Cotswolds for a few years until I had my first son. Life up until this point had been all about my career and suddenly (as much as we had longed and planned for a baby), it was turned upside down. I was struggling, some days I wondered if everyone around me would be better off if I wasn't there anymore. I isolated myself and my confidence dropped to an all-time low. I felt like I wasn't good enough for anything. But, with the help and support from friends and family I managed to pull myself up and out of that feeling.

Then, one day I came across the Prince's Trust. They were supporting people who wanted to set up in business. I decided to go for it, I put together a business plan and approached them with my cake business idea. I was successful and they loaned me £2,000. Best of all, they provided me with a business mentor - a local businesswoman who helped with accounts, strategies, and contacts. I started to work from home, baking and building the business by attending every school fete, church fair, and food festival going. I talked to everyone who would listen to me and taste my cakes. I was then invited to speak at a large chamber meeting; I couldn't say no to this opportunity and let the shy girl win. I stood up in front of 300 people (mainly men in grey suits) and nervously talked about my business. Half way though I realised that I knew more about my business that they did, so I relaxed and enjoyed it. From that point onwards, I went to every conference I could get to.

One day, I was at the Women in Rural Enterprise and there was a reporter from the Sunday times conducting a talk. I ran up to her at the end, shoved my business card in her hand, and told her a little about my business. A few weeks later she was doing an article on small businesses and I had a quarter page article in the Sunday

Times. A couple of months into the business while planning with my mentor, she suggested I get in touch with the palace about making a cake for Prince Charles. The palace suggested I made a cake for TRH The Prince of Wales and The Duchess of Cornwall to celebrate their first wedding anniversary. I carefully planned, baked, and decorated many cakes until I found the perfect design - a chocolate cake finished with chocolate petals. I delivered the cake and had a lovely letter back saying how much they had enjoyed it.

The business grew from strength to strength and began to outgrow my home kitchen. I hired church kitchens and started supplying local delis, cafés, and restaurants. I entered the Great Taste Awards and won two which was great PR for the business. My second son came along three years after my first and an hour after giving birth I was on the phone checking orders had been delivered! The business continued to grow organically while I had the best job of being a mum to two boys. Once my first son started school and my second started nursery, I decided it was time to fulfil my lifelong dream of owning a cake shop. I found premises in a lovely area of Leamington Spa, put a full bakery in the back of the shop, and took on a business partner. I had always wanted the smell of fresh baking to float down the street, to bring people in with their noses. And it worked! We opened the cake emporium with patisserie creations; cheesecakes, chocolate tarts, cupcakes, handmade chocolates, and of course cakes for weddings and celebrations. The shop was a roaring success straight away and we were welcomed into the community. We were invited onto a show called Britain's Best Bakery for ITV, it was sold as a Bake Off style show for professionals which we would film in our shop. 40 hours of filming turned into 20 minutes of screen time on a prime-time ITV show. Once it was aired people from all over the country started visiting - a family came all the way from Newcastle just to buy our brownies, and we had emails from all over the world asking for our recipes!

A couple of years in we decided to open a second shop in Kenilworth. The second shop was full of hope and excitement to be the gateway to the growth of our business. Except it wasn't;

Kenilworth was a very different town, with different consumers, and no kitchen onsite. It broke even, but it took more time and energy and split us in two which didn't help our first store. But I desperately didn't want to fail, so we continued plugging away with it.

We had a call from The Alan Tichmarsh Show, they were doing a show all about The Prince's Trust and wanted me to decorate a cake live on air four days away. Of course, I said yes! A day before we were due to film they called again to ask me if I could make a cake for Phillip Scofield and present it to him live on air! Again - YES! These opportunities don't come around every day. The day of the filming was quite an experience; I had my make-up done sitting in between Elaine Paige and David Essex, the green room had Bear Grills, Gino Di Campo, and of course Phillip Scofield who was a dream!

A little while later, my business partner went on maternity leave and decided she wanted to stay at home with her beautiful daughter, and so didn't return. At the same time, my marriage broke down so I decided to close the second store in Kenilworth and concentrate on getting though this terrible time for me and my boys. I applied for a business course taught at Aston Business School, the places were seriously limited and we had to present to be accepted on the course which was funded by Goldman Sachs.

I was accepted and had the steepest four months of learning in my life. It transformed me and my business and got me looking at it completely differently. I put a great manager in the store and took some time away for myself, and returned with renewed vigour. I decided to open Leamington's first dessert parlour. We changed a few things around and started making freakshakes (extreme milkshakes), ice-cream desserts, hot puddings, and more of our famous cheesecakes. We had a great launch and people loved what we were doing. Except I didn't. I was spending my time recruiting, dealing with staff issues, shopping, delivering, ordering, and pretty much doing everything apart from making cakes, which was what I started the business to do. I had employed and trained two pastry chefs, and they were doing the job I loved. So, I made a tough decision to strip the business right back. By this point there were

64 coffee shops in the local area and we were supplying a lot of them and competing with ourselves, so I decided to close the café side of the business. I wanted to be known as the cake specialist that I had started the business 12 years earlier to do. It was a huge relief, I had been chasing growth and losing sight of what I loved about my business. A year on and I had turned the business into a something much more manageable and profitable.

In 2016 I won Entrepreneur of the year at The Woman Who... Awards. I was chuffed beyond words. For someone else to pick me as a leader in business was a massive pat on the back to that little girl who had no belief in herself. So, from then on I decided to have faith in myself. I have learnt so much though my 13 years in business, how to do things, and how not to do things, but I don't regret a single thing.

In January 2017 I had the first New Year's Eve off in 20 years. My partner and I went away for a few days. I stood at the top of the Giant's Causeway and realised it was now or never to make a change for me and my family. Standing in the roaring wind overlooking the wild Atlantic I realised I had been living to work; working 60-70 hours per week, working weekends and school holidays. My business and my values no longer lined up.

I made the terrifying decision to sell Sweet As in search for a better life for me and my children, and on the 19th of January 2018 I signed over the shop to a local cake maker so I could start my new life...

Jenny's top tip:

"Surround yourself with the right people.
Keep on pushing. Research. Innovate. Believe. And
most of all, if your passion disappears, reinvent or
move on. Life is too short to keep doing something
you don't love."

Jenny's favourite quote:

"If you always do what you've always done,
you will always get what you've always got."

Albert Einstein

TWITTER NAME:
@Jennyhudson4

Ruth Mary Chipperfield
MChem DipLCM

JEWELLERY SCULPTOR AND FOUNDER
RUTH MARY JEWELLERY

"

RUNNING A BUSINESS IS ALL ABOUT
BEING CALM, WHILST IN THE MIDDLE
OF THE STORM AND LEARNING WHEN
YOU'RE RIGHT ON THE CLIFF EDGE.

RUTH MARY CHIPPERFIELD
MChem DipLCM
RUTH MARY JEWELLERY

Today, I am the jewellery designer and founder of Ruth Mary Jewellery. Five years ago, my identity was much more bound up in ill health. However, this is not designed to be a sob story, or even a sad story with a happy ending, but an honest account of my journey through some tough years of illness, which were littered with blessings and extraordinary circumstances that have lead me to this point.

In December 2009 at the age of just 20, and having been at University for only 10 weeks, I married my best friend, Paul Chipperfield. We grinned as we promised to stand by each other 'in sickness and in health'. Less than a year later I was diagnosed with narcolepsy. This is a condition which leaves the person severely sleep deprived, as their body constantly oscillates between sleep and wakefulness, without ever giving the body the rest it needs. A 'normal' person (what is normal anyway?) will experience a certain amount of deep sleep during the night, and they are awake during the day. Somebody with narcolepsy experiences mostly dream sleep (also called REM sleep) and will often do so for only a few seconds or minutes at a time. The result is extreme sleep deprivation, so the sufferer regularly falls asleep regardless of where they are in any given moment. While asleep, the person will wake up, and while awake, they fall asleep. An oscillation cycle that should last 24 hours lasts only a few minutes or seconds.

I was in my second year of my Chemistry degree at Warwick University when I was first diagnosed. By the time I was stable on my new prescription drugs, I had missed half the academic years' worth of lectures. Prior to this point, my attempt at self-medication consisted of six shots of espresso in one go to get me though one hour of study. I should have gone back a year, but by the grace of God, I began to love learning the subject and caught up by working extremely long hours each day.

Health was still a daily struggle, but I did well in my exams and with my third year ahead, what could possibly go wrong?

Well, a lot. My condition became so bad that my consultant remarked that he had never seen anybody with more severe symptoms. The amount of time I needed to sleep in each 24-hour cycle increased to 18 hours. I also developed another symptom, called cataplexy. This meant my body would lose muscle tone and I would collapse to the floor, unable to move, whilst maintaining full consciousness. Perhaps because I never do things by halves in life, this happened over 30 times a day and one attack could last between a few seconds and two hours.

Before long it was unsafe for me to leave the house without a carer. So, in 'sickness and in health', Paul stepped into this role. I walked away from my academic career after clinging on for as long as I could. I thought I would be able to return to my degree a few months later, after I became aware of a so-called 'wonder-drug' for narcolepsy sufferers. To manufacture it is extremely simple. Combine two substances (gamma-hydroxyburyrate and sodium hydroxide) under gentle heat and some laboratory kit, and you're done. No filtration, no crystallisation needed. Chemistry lesson over! My point is, it's an incredibly simple medication to produce. However, this 'wonder-drug' costs £13,000 a year for the NHS due to licensing issues. You can imagine my temptation as a chemist-in-the-know to make it myself, and I could have done so for just £70 a year. What stopped me was the fact that this is illegal. This potentially life-altering medication just so happens to be the so-called 'date-rape' drug.

So, I had no other choice but to take the arduous route of demonstrating to the NHS that I was an exceptional case; this process involved three applications and appeals and took a whole year; but finally, having fought hard as a family, we were granted the funding on the eve of my 22nd birthday.

I started to think of all the things that I would suddenly be able to do with ease, like choosing when to get up and not having to wait two hours before relieving myself because my body chose not to move. It was an unbelievable feeling, the first time I took this narcotic liquid – it knocks the user out so they get deep sleep and are then awake the next day. For the first time I could remember in years and years, I actually felt awake! If this was what normal health was like then it would be amazing!

Sadly, this feeling didn't last. What was unknown to me, to my medical consultant, and also to a large number of medical professionals, is the importance of REM sleep in conjunction with deep sleep. For 20 years my body received a lot of REM sleep (or dream sleep), which serves to recharge the mind and bring emotional closure to our experiences from that day. Upon receiving the new drug, I switched to having only deep sleep and no REM sleep – and I was about to experience a whole new world of illness.

Whilst physically I felt better than ever, my mental health rapidly deteriorated. As I could no longer mentally recharge by processing the day's experience through dream sleep, I had a sensory overload. For over a year I had not left the house alone and Paul had done everything for me. I had forgotten what it was like to go out alone, interact in public, organise a shopping list, clean, cook, make plans, work, and countless other tasks. I hadn't even been an adult for long and now I had to learn it all over again.

With extreme sensory overload and no REM sleep, the perfect storm was brewing. At first I just didn't 'feel right', which I would just put down to getting used to my new medication. Then I began to feel more and more uncomfortable. I managed to drown these feelings out by pretending the anxiety was actually excitement for my new business ventures, but my thinking was completely clouded.

Then one day, when I couldn't maintain my strenuous state of excitement and emotional arousal, everything unravelled. I experienced psychotic episodes, began hearing voices that weren't real and developed intense depression. My first thought of every day was that I wanted to die. My last thought of the day was that I wanted to die. This lasted for months. Occasionally I experienced a day when I was able to mask everything with excitement, declaring to the world that 'it was all over' and 'I was fine now'. The next day the nightmare returned, but each time it was worse.

I lost almost a third of my body weight in three to four months. Have you ever heard of people visiting A&E unnecessarily with stomach pain? I was one of those people. Convinced something awful was happening, it was an emergency. Little did I know that everything was triggered inside my mind. As my physical body became weaker and weaker, no-one around me knew enough to suggest that it might be my body's response to a troubled mind. I now know that our brain makes no distinction between a perceived threat and an actual one. It sets the 'fight or flight' response into action regardless, at which point our body is pumped full of adrenaline and our heart and breathing rate increases. Our cognitive function, ability to remember things, digestive function, and everything else we are normally able to do, shuts down. We're now in survival mode and so is every cell in our body. When we maintain this state for long periods of time, it affects our entire being; not just our mental health; but also our physical heath.

While all this was going on, I continued my attempts to build a business. Before I received my 'wonder-drug', I had spent some of my few wakeful hours making costume jewellery. It had been a hobby since childhood and together Paul and I gradually developed a collection. Paul is a talented illustrator and creative designer, so our skills seemed to complement each other. The concept was simple. Paul designed little intricate patterns inside circles, which he printed onto photo paper. These were then cut out, placed inside a silver plated setting and finished with a glass dome to magnify the pattern. This allowed us to create a range of jewellery, such as necklaces, earrings and so on.

Shortly after receiving the drug, I attended an antique fair, where my mum suggested I purchase a little plastic item called a 'tatting shuttle', used for lace making. 'You can teach yourself, you'll enjoy using it', she said. So I spent my two pounds and found out how to do it via YouTube. I've never liked copying other people's designs, so I developed my own.

The pivotal moment in my business direction came when I discovered that moulds can be made around objects. Now, lace is a delicate object, and one of the more complicated things to make moulds from. But with my mental health declining, I didn't think much of investing the rest of our savings into commissioning some moulds to be made – there was no guarantee they would even cast successfully. Neither did I think much of having the lace replicated in sterling silver, despite the fact I had never learnt silversmithing. In my mind I could just attach little jump rings to the components and link them together like I had done with costume jewellery. I had no idea that I would have to saw excess silver off the silver lace pieces, file it to recreate the texture of the lace and polish it. Then I would need to solder all sorts of components together to create the finished jewellery. With this trial-and-error approach, I simply purchased another piece of equipment when one piece of kit didn't do the job properly – this resulted in quite an outlay. In time however, I did build quite an extensive work bench; one that I now benefit from, I'm pleased to say. However, throughout this time of learning and investing, my mental health was declining – I didn't actually have any notion of how I was going to market and sell this high-end jewellery to make any money to live on.

So it was certainly an unconventional way to start a business, but I still believe that if I had been mentally aware of what I was actually doing, I would never have had the courage to take those steps.

Eventually our savings dried up, I returned to University and Paul was able to start freelancing. I had taken three years out of my degree, but I was determined to finish it. With the jewellery business not really going anywhere, this seemed like the best option. My health remained a serious struggle, and I was constantly trying to balance the side effects of the drug with the need to take a certain dosage of it to stay awake.

I finished my third and fourth year, but only found out

afterwards why I had found it such a struggle. My drug dose had been lowered significantly by the end of my studies, compared to previously – something that was in no small part facilitated by an enormous amount of prayer and support from friends and family. I graduated with a grade I wasn't entirely happy with, and because I would never have the health to hold down a 'proper job', I went back to the flexibility of the jewellery business, which had been ticking over on the side for a little while.

Working from home did, however, amplify some of my mental struggles, especially the episodes of paranoia. After a few months my sister very kindly offered to pay for psychotherapy, which has proved a huge turning point. It was only at this point that I discovered post traumatic stress disorder, and began to be equipped to unlock all the scenarios that would act as emotional triggers throughout the day.

One of my main ambitions for the business is to build a global luxury fashion brand, one that employs people who might need a second (or third, or fourth...) chance in life, including those with physical and mental illnesses. I realised that my determination to work whilst navigating both of these has been a training ground to equip me to help others in the future.

In 2017 I began to see the business and my personal confidence grow. The Prince's Trust gave me a loan for my business, which helped get things off the ground.

Sales and commissions began coming in, and I even accepted a commission for a men's gold wedding ring. My precious metal lace designs are now my signature style and it's what I'm known for. Occasionally I enjoy taking on slightly different work, using more traditional metalsmithing techniques. However, I usually stick to creating precious metal lace, by first hand stitching the design in cotton to create a bespoke shape. Once my customer approves it, I create a mould around the lace and recreate it in silver or gold. I've had some wonderful bridal commissions, whereby I've created silver lace jewellery to match the wedding dress.

This new era of social media has caused me to abandon the

traditional concept of two major spring/summer and autumn/winter collections. Instead, I involve my customers and audience in my design process. This helpfully integrates the market research side of things.

In October 2017 I won an award for, 'Successful Career from Home', from the Warwickshire-based Ladies First networking group. The timing couldn't have been more significant, as it was one year on from undertaking psychotherapy. The contrast was clearly visible, as only 12 months previously, I had been terrified of being in my own house. As a result of this and lots of other networking, I have had the privilege of being asked to speak on radio and at a number of events – sometimes sharing my story.

I was even chosen by The Guardian as one of the top 100 UK small businesses, and I was invited to Number 10 Downing Street (unfortunately Mrs May was absent!).

As my Ruth Mary Jewellery has evolved, Paul has been instrumental in developing the brand using his skills as a designer. Simply put, I would never be where I am now without his graphic design skills. I am now stocked in five shops, including in London and the Birmingham Jewellery Quarter. I have also been selected to exhibit at Desire Fair in Kensington in March 2018, which is one of the most prestigious jewellery events in the UK.

I have never taken any courses in jewellery making, but am proud to be completely self-taught. I've always found visualisation in three dimensions easier than two dimensions, which has therefore informed my sculptural approach to jewellery design.

One of the biggest challenges I sometimes observe creative entrepreneurs facing is an inability to emotionally detach themselves from a creation that has had so much time and energy invested. I found laying my jewellery business to one side before returning to University a real emotional struggle, especially as I had to admit that it wasn't working at the time. However, getting used to establishing a means of emotional detachment has been a real blessing. It means I am now able make much better, objective business decisions now, than if it had succeeded financially the first time round.

So I will end with this: Don't let failure be final, but make every stumble a foothold for climbing even higher.

Ruth's top tip:

"Don't believe every thought that pops into your mind. Worry is a negative use of the imagination. Therefore, the battles of life aren't played out in the environment around you, but in your mind."

Ruth's favourite quote:

"There's nothing wrong with speaking your mind, so long as your mind is in a suitable condition."

By Alan Wilson

(my driving instructor from when I was age 17)

www.ruthmary.com

TWITTER NAME:
@R_M_Jewellery

Sally Dhillon

CO-FOUNDER
CAREER-MUMS PARTNERSHIP

"

GIVE YOURSELF PERMISSION TO CREATE YOUR
FUTURE, TAKE ACTION AND SHINE BRIGHTLY.

SALLY DHILLON
CAREER-MUMS PARTNERSHIP

Back in December 2014, I was feeling sorry for myself being almost house bound having had surgery on my foot to remove a painful bunion. I invited my new neighbour around for a coffee to get to know each other (hoping that she'd offer to help out with the school run whilst I was out of action!). It was lovely to have new neighbours with younger children as we'd moved into a small family community with much older children.

We got chatting and realised that we had many things in common, in addition to young children. Nishi was taking a career break and was just finishing a coaching qualification; I'd had quite a lengthy career break and was an experienced coach. We'd both moved to the Coventry & Warwickshire area to be closer to our respective husband's families, even though both our husbands were working most days in London.

A few coffees later, and with a recovered foot, we talked a lot about our frustrations of wanting to find work that was enjoyable and fulfilling, whilst fitting around school hours. We both recognised that during our career breaks, we had lost confidence, contacts and a sense of who we were. My husband's tongue-in-cheek answer was to get a part-time job at our local café... our response was quite different. We reasoned that if we were experiencing difficulties, then other people must be too – and with our combined experience we could do something about it... and so Career-Mums was born!

We spent plenty of time discussing ideas, doing research and dreaming. It was encouraging to find that others had already started to see the need to support women back to work and there were a few examples of similar offerings particularly around London and the Home Counties. We did some market testing and then designed our own return to work programme. We decided to run a free pilot and contacted friends to get involved as guinea pigs... we had just one taker and lots of firm 'no's from other friends. We ditched the pilot!

Not to be deterred, we carried on and in January 2016 we ran our first Return to Work workshop programme with six lovely ladies. We had managed to coerce some friends, mums from the school gates, and having put a small ad in the local newspaper, we had one lady who had returned to the area after a 30 year absence following her husband's career around the world whilst raising her family.

We worked hard to create a fantastic workshop experience and the results and feedback were amazing. By the third and final workshop we had one woman arrive with a dramatic new hairstyle and another wearing a new business suit. All were standing taller, looking proud and excited about their futures. They'd all developed their own unique relaunch plan, re-found their confidence and were engaged in creating their own bright futures. From that first group of stay at home mums one became a nutritional therapist, one launched a training business, another secured a part-time marketing job (she has since been promoted and gone on to even bigger and better things!), and a lady who decided to take her new wedding business idea seriously and get set up for the new season. Their dreams were becoming a reality; their families were fully on board and they'd worked through whatever it was that was stopping them doing it.

Our plan, our big idea had worked. Our confidence was growing too. I certainly felt like I was getting my 'mojo' back. We marketed the next workshop but didn't get any takers... we quickly realised that there was no such thing as an overnight success and we were targeting women who were quite difficult to reach. If we were to make this a viable business we needed to get serious, invest in marketing know-how and broaden our reach to offer services to employers too.

After all, if women are finding it difficult to find suitable work especially after taking more than a standard maternity leave, then this adds up to so much lost talent. Therefore, shouldn't employers be doing more to tap into the talent and experience that is out there? We had a website developed to market our services to both mums and employers offering services such as maternity coaching, returnships, consultancy, and line manager training – all to help employers attract and retain female talent alongside our relaunch your career workshops.

I became very aware of the disadvantages that many women face in the workplace and how motherhood can impact on our career progression and earnings potential. I was angry. I felt a very strong desire to do something about it. I felt as though I had found my purpose, my calling, my mission – whatever you want to call it – and I felt ready to be let loose on the world to make a positive difference.

I'm a thinker... I'm curious about the world and I love making connections... I now think that I was destined to do this work and so many things in my life had led me to this point.

I was raised in Yorkshire to quite young parents in a traditional working-class family. I spent a lot of time with my paternal Grandma who was a strong woman and professional housewife. Monday was washing day, Tuesday cleaning day, Wednesday baking day, etc. She had a very close friendship with her sisters who met regularly in the afternoons once the housework was finished. A true sisterhood. I never had a sister – just one brother, 18 months younger than me. He was bright, intelligent, sporty – the heir to the family throne. Not much was expected of me, apart from helping out around the house; I was being trained to be a lovely housewife when I grew up!

My parents were heavily influenced by some of their friends with older daughters – they had very strong views about educating girls being a waste of time beyond 16 and that the ideal roles for girls were to work in a bank or be a secretary. My mum even sent me to night school when I was 14 to learn how to type! I took my school work seriously and worked hard to scrape reasonable grades, all while having my Grandma say things like, 'I don't know why you want to be studying those books, I'd much rather be washing the floor!'

I didn't know what I wanted for my future, I was a very shy and compliant girl but I didn't see myself fitting into other people's notions of what I should be doing.

I managed to make a significant move when I was 16 and instead of staying at my school's sixth form, I went with a small group of friends to a Sixth Form College, 12 miles away from home. We were seen as rebels! After a few months, I met my first boyfriend. His family had very different views on the value of education (and educating girls) from my family – his elder sister was doing a PhD. The relationship didn't last, but his family's influence was immense. For the first time, I believed I could achieve academically and there was no reason why I couldn't carry on, be the first girl in my family to go to University and get a degree – even if my mum was busy scouring the job adverts in the local newspaper trying to find me a secretarial job the night before I got my A-level results!

Anyway, I went to Leeds University, studied Economics and gained a new-found appreciation for life and learning having spent most of my four year degree working in a city-centre bar.

After graduating I decided to pursue a career in HR (or personnel, as it was known then) – I'm not sure why, but there was something about the power of deciding whether someone got offered a job or not that was quite appealing.

I worked for a large food retailer, then a fashion retailer. I completed a Master's degree in Human Resources Management. I'd moved to London – initially for a three month project but ended up staying for 16 years. By my late 20s, I had developed a reputation for taking on roles that no one else wanted to do. I quickly realised the value of short-term projects, maternity covers and secondments to different parts of the business and the impact they could have on my career, experience and influence. I saw opportunities where others didn't.

When I was 30, I decided I wanted to broaden out of retailing and ideally get a job in the city where there might be a better chance of meeting Mr Right. Time was moving on, my biological clock was ticking, and I wanted to settle down like a lot of my friends had started to do. After a number of interviews with investment firms, I decided that the HR roles I was applying for were quite limited in terms of their influence, and instead I took a role with a manufacturing conglomerate where I would also be able to get more international experience.

By 31, I met my husband-to-be and by 33 I was appointed to be HR Director of a building management systems subsidiary. All was going well. We wanted to start a family. But nothing happened. We tried lots of different things to get pregnant. Nothing happened. I changed things at work to work from home more, reducing my travel time and eventually only worked four days per week to reduce stress. And still nothing happened. A reorganisation at work meant that I was asked to take on responsibility for another operation which would have increased my travel and time away from home, which I didn't want to do... so I managed to agree leaving arrangements and decided to work freelance.

By this time, we were having fertility investigations and treatments. And still nothing happened. I also had some excellent coaching on setting up my own business and decided quite quickly that I wanted to retrain to become a coach too. I spent over a year absorbed in studying, learning and practicing becoming an Executive Coach and Leadership Development trainer, securing associate work with a fabulous coaching company. I had excellent clients, for the first time a whole female work team, and plenty of flexibility to attend medical appointments and do everything I could to support my body to get pregnant.

Eventually we started IVF treatment and after a few false starts, our first full cycle worked! Our first baby was conceived in a test tube in a lab just by London's Borough Market. We were absolutely thrilled and could finally put our plans into action to move to the Midlands to be closer to both our extended families and raise our much-longed for family. So, in the summer of 2005 we moved to the country and welcomed our first daughter into the world.

It was quite tough moving to a new area, and being a new mum was so joyful and yet so tough. I felt isolated and unsure of myself as a mother. I also felt quite bored, but quickly got to know a group of fellow new mums and created foundations around our new home. I remember, not long after my daughter was born, my husband returning to work and going out for drinks with colleagues one evening. I was so resentful of his ability to just go, carry on with his life and not have to worry about what time he came home, whereas I was no more than a milking machine with no life of my own anymore.

After a few months, I started to pick up bits of freelance work that I could manage around sleep-times and also started working with some new coaching clients. The best of both worlds – plenty of time to be mum and also the opportunity to continue doing what I absolutely loved in my coaching work. My newly-retired parents would come and stay with us for a few days and take over the running of the house and childcare whilst I worked.

I was approaching my late 30s and we knew that we wanted at least one more child to complete our family. We went straight back to the IVF route that had worked for us already, whilst knowing that our chances of getting pregnant were significantly reducing. We had three torturous and unsuccessful rounds of IVF and following our consultant's advice, decided to stop there.

Devastated and drained - it brought it home to us how precious our first miracle baby was, but we still didn't feel that our dream of having a larger family was over and after a short while we decided to look into adoption.

In the meantime, I continued my love of learning and started studying organisational psychology with an amazing teacher in Oxford. I took a weekend each month to spend in Oxford and absorb myself in learning and connecting – I found it such a contrast to my life as a mum. After the recession, most of our corporate clients had had their budgets cut for external coaches, and most of my client work stopped.

We were eventually invited to an information evening by our local adoption agency, followed by intensive preparation sessions before our assessment to become adoptive parents started. Nine months later we were approved and matched with a little girl who had just turned one. She was the perfect addition to our family, which had also grown further with the addition of a puppy. As part of the adoption process, one of us had to commit to being at home with our new daughter full-time for at least the first year. I got the gig!

In fact, I ended up staying at home with her until she was fully settled at school. During this time, I busied myself with volunteering for PTA duties and becoming a freelance trainer and parent consultant for Adoption UK, a nationwide charity that supports adoptive parents. Never one for going to the gym, I also went to painting classes and started learning to play the saxophone whilst my little one was in nursery and reception, but I yearned to be able to use my coaching and training skills along with my business knowledge.

I had had the privilege and luxury of being a stay at home mum. It had taken over ten years to create the family that we wanted – and the cost of this was my career. My husband's career was flying, continuing on an upward trajectory. I finally plucked up the courage to apply for a role working at a local Business School – a job that I was more than qualified for, and despite there being lots of applicants and getting through to the final stage, I was heartbroken when it wasn't offered to me – I felt old, washed-up and worthless.

And so when Nishi and I met - when we shared our experiences of having a career break and when we decided to do something about it, I had a rich tapestry of experiences to pull on – my upbringing, my education, my HR work, my coaching and training work, my business leadership experience, my psychology studies as well as my own parenting experience and supporting other families with very complex needs.

Four out of five women taking maternity leave report that they feel discriminated against by their employer; the gender pay gap in the West Midlands is running at around 24%; there are still more FTSE100 CEOs called David than there are female CEOs; and we have a significant skills shortage in this country. Having a child and/or taking a career break should not be the end of your career or your career potential.

After that initial workshop programme, and seeing those women feel like they had a purpose again, I knew that there was a need for the work that we were doing. It also felt great to be leading sessions again and using my experience. Nishi and I set about developing our Career-Mums service and getting our business known locally.

We keep a very close eye on what the big corporates, the government, and our competitors are doing. We see the drivers out in the market – the government's voluntary targets to get more women onto FTSE Boards, the introduction of gender pay gap reporting for larger employers this year, the growing understanding that increased diversity is good for business, the high profile #metoo and #timesup campaigns along with Women's marches. Its 100 years since women got the vote in the UK, but we're certainly a long way from having equality of opportunity.

We use our professional experience to support local employers to be more attractive to all working parents – flexible and smarter working initiatives, maternity coaching, and unconscious bias training.

We've also seen the need to do something to develop more women leaders locally and we now run regular Developing Women Leaders workshops to educate about the need to think differently about how we develop leadership talent in women. We're also introducing Leadership Development Coaching.

Having a successful career is not about working long hours to climb up a sticky, alien corporate ladder – having a successful career and being a leader that makes a difference comes in many different guises and we're here to help you re-write the rule books. It's time to stop the maternity penalty.

As women, it's important to stand up and make sure our voices are heard. Volunteer for new projects, take opportunities to speak, support one another, ask for whatever it is that you want, and be a role model for the next generation. I've stepped up to take on a leadership role in our local CIPD branch of 2,500 local HR professionals and I intend to continue to learn, grow, evolve and inspire.

And at the heart of our business will always be the help we give to women to relaunch their careers, whether supporting a return to employment, starting their own business, or retraining after a career break. We are the return to work experts.

Our Career-Mums mission is to contribute to the removal of the gender barriers to career and business success.

My personal mission, as a mum, is to do this for my girls.

And finally, I'm glad to say that my parents' views on education have shifted along with the times and, with five granddaughters, they're enjoying them growing up and seeing what they become. And my brother, well he's proudly worked in banking for over 30 years!

Sally's top tip:

"Understand why you are doing what you are doing. Knowing your 'why' will keep you motivated, tap into your passion and help you be authentic. Your business may be a long-held dream or have come from a seemingly impromptu idea; you may consider it planned, fate or your destiny. It's likely to have its roots in your past. If you feel lost, overwhelmed or as though you are not getting anywhere, always return to your 'why'. If you are unsure of your 'why', work with a coach to help you explore your purpose and motivation."

Sally's favourite quote:

"Be the change you wish to see in the World."

Gandhi

www.career-mums.co.uk

TWITTER NAME:
@SallyDhillon @career_mums

Erica Kemp

MEMBER/OWNER
FAMILY LAWYER AND HEAD OF THE FAMILY DEPARTMENT
ALSTERS KELLEY

"

YOU NEED TO TAKE CARE OF YOURSELF.
TRY TO ENJOY EVERY DAY AND LAUGH EVEN
WHEN THINGS ARE GOING AWRY.

ERICA KEMP // ALSTERS KELLEY

ERICA   KEMP
ALSTERS   KELLEY

It is a real privilege to be given the opportunity to tell people about my business and life to date. Along the way I have acquired two husbands (the second much better than the first!), two step sons, one daughter, two cats, a dog, and a quarter share in the law firm Alsters Kelley LLP.

I didn't start off my business life as a Lawyer. A long time ago I studied for a History Degree at Aberystwyth University. Being from a Welsh background with a strong family tradition of producing teachers, I then spent a year training as a teacher, only to discover very quickly that was not what I wanted to do, and I suspect it was not what the pupils wanted me to do either!

During my time at school and during the university holidays, I had worked as a Saturday girl for Boots the Chemist and I found that I really enjoyed the products, the customers, and the excitement of working in a commercially challenging and target driven environment. The manager of the branch that I was working in after finishing my degree suggested, somewhat to my surprise, that retailing might provide a suitable career for a History Graduate!

It transpired that indeed it was. I was offered a place as a Graduate Trainee with Habitat, which was at that time, a very exciting and innovative retailer under the close control and direction of Terence Conran. I started working in the Habitat stores and ended up spending Mr Conran's money on products for the store group as a member of the buying team.

As you might imagine, it was wonderful working closely with product designers and manufacturers, handling a substantial buying budget, exploring market trends, travelling to trade fairs and suppliers both in the UK and abroad, and occasionally facing the terrifying prospect of making product presentations to Terence Conran himself.

I remained in retail buying with a number of high street retailers, with my last retail role being with another innovative retail concept: Matalan. However, in 1996 my daughter was born and suddenly the prospect of international travel seemed somewhat less attractive. At the time I was living in Chester near the College of Law and I made the decision to change my career and to retrain as a Lawyer. This was something that had always seemed of interest to me, and I found studying and caring for a new baby at the same time stimulating, terrifying, and demanding all in equal proportions.

Fortunately, my daughter was a really good baby and I found a wonderful nursery who provided me as a new mother with as much care and support as they provided to my daughter!

The academic work during the two years at the College of Law was very challenging but I passed the exams (with commendations!) and was then lucky to secure a Training Contract with a local firm in Chester.

Following my husband's change of work, it became necessary to move from Chester to the Midlands and I moved to work for the firm that I now co-own with three colleagues, Alsters Kelley, joining them in 2002. Alsters Kelley is one of the largest Solicitors firm in Warwickshire and the West Midlands with offices in Coventry, Leamington, Nuneaton and Southam.

We offer expertise in a number of areas of law; I work in Family Law dealing primarily with divorce and financial matters arising from relationship breakdown. A considerable amount of our work in this area focusses on advising clients in relation to the future childcare after relationships fail. As a firm, Alsters Kelley also offer advice in respect of Wills and Trusts and Probate to clients that have suffered Clinical Negligence, private individuals purchasing domestic property, and also to people seeking to purchase commercial property. We advise clients' disputes of a legal nature between individuals such as boundary disputes, employment issues, contentious probate, etc.

We remain proud to offer access to justice for a very diverse array of clients. We are one of very few firms that have continued to offer assistance to some of the most vulnerable clients in society through Legal Aid.

Providing Legal Aid is onerous administratively and the rates of pay are very low. However, as a Firm we feel that it is so important that we continue to provide assistance to people that would otherwise suffer not just financial hardship, but significant distress. The majority of the Legal Aid work we undertake involves representing children and parents in care proceedings. We believe that ensuring parents and children in such circumstances have access to legal advice is not only critical to the fairness of the process, but is also important to broader society.

We aim to ensure that all of our clients, however their legal costs are funded, find our Lawyers and staff to be kind, helpful, and excellent. We employ around 91 members of staff and the business is owned and run by myself alongside three fellow members. Our turnover is around £4 million, and it is challenging and rewarding to work both as a Lawyer and to play a full-time part in the running of a multimillion pound business. We always remain acutely aware of the responsibility that we as business owners owe, not only to ourselves and our families, but also to every single member of staff who are reliant on us to make a success of this business.

I was made a Partner in Alsters Kelley in 2006 and discovered very quickly the enormity of the challenges that faced the business. Becoming a partner in a law firm exposes the partners to liabilities which generally don't arise, for instance in respect of Directors of Limited Companies. In a Partnership the partners are liable financially and otherwise for everything that goes on within the business. There is no limited liability and with hindsight I could and should have taken independent advice about the business before investing in it and taking on such a substantial liability, the extent of which was not at all clear at the time.

Aside from approaching partnership with what now appears to be a ludicrous level of naivety and trust, I quickly discovered there were fundamental and serious structural issues with the business. Firstly, there were far too many partners for the turnover. It is the ratio of partners to turnover which determines the levels of drawings available (or not!) to the partners based on share of profit. To say that this was a painful lesson is a significant understatement and the financial consequences of the decision to join the partnership in 2006 remain. The second thing that became clear very quickly was that the business was under capitalised and as a result had been borrowing money to support cashflow. This created a cycle that was very difficult to break, as repayment of borrowing created its own cash pressure.

The legal profession is very heavily regulated (rightly so) and it became clear that the business needed to review and sharpen up its business policies and procedures to ensure compliance with regulatory requirements breaches which can (again, rightly so) prove fatal for a law firm.

In 2008 two of the founding partners of Alsters Kelley left and those of us remaining took the opportunity to address these issues that were holding the business back. Then, also in 2008, came the recession and for a firm that was heavily dependent on domestic conveyancing and commercial property work, this downturn in the economy and the collapse of the housing market brought additional and very unwelcome challenges.

So, what did we do? Having considered running for the hills and deciding that wasn't the answer we set to work to stabilise the business, rectify the structural problems and address the very serious cash position which caused all of us, as members, a number of sleepless nights.

This is what we did...

1. We restructured the business, reducing the number of partners from thirteen to five, so that the ratio of partner to turnover was more reasonable and appropriate. Best of all, we managed the reduction of partners amicably with only one of the

former partners leaving the business and the others remaining within Alsters Kelley. Indeed, we still have two former partners in the firm, the others either having retired from the profession or moved to other jobs on good terms.

2.   As Members we took some difficult decisions about our own personal and financial commitment to the business. Could we...should we... put our future financial and professional futures at risk in order to do what needed to be done to ensure the survival of the business? It was often very scary but we were all totally committed to making the business succeed.

3.   We worked with our bank in an open and cooperative relationship. This was occasionally (or more than occasionally) painful, but when the business reviews were proposed we found that they were in fact helpful. They confirmed the viability of the business and noted the commitment and competence of us as managers and owners of the business. A great confidence boost. But they also highlighted areas of concern, challenging us to look at our business model and question our core assumptions.

4.   As a result of the business review we made the decision to focus our business on offering legal advice to private individuals rather than to businesses. We sold our company commercial business to a local competitor firm and the sale of that work eased some of the cash flow pressures.

5.   Although we had a constructive relationship with our bank, when the recession really started to impact the economy the banks lost their appetite to lend, and that was a real issue for us as we grappled with a business that was overburdened with borrowing.

We continued to struggle with cash flow partly because of reduced revenues due to the recession but also as a result of this antecedent debt. It became clear that we needed to look at some radical options to survive if the bank was no longer going to provide the level of support the business needed.

We were approached by several possible merger or buy out partners, but ultimately and quite unexpectedly the answer came from a speculative meeting with an American investment fund who were considering dipping their toes into the UK legal market. They liked what they saw, and they made an investment in the business in 2013 and remain a supportive but very hands off partner.

So where are we now?

1.   We have a stable business with cash flow under control, which is profitable.

2.   We remain focused on providing kind, helpful and excellent service to private individuals.

3.   We are very much grounded and involved in our local area, sponsoring local charities and supporting events such as Woman Who... last year, and have continued to actively sponsor.

4.   We are embracing the opportunity to develop young talent through the apprenticeship scheme, working closely with Warwickshire College. We have a real track record in developing people internally with several Lawyers having joined as junior staff and worked their way up through the ranks. Some 40% of our staff have been with the firm for more than 10 years.

5.   We have worked closely with an industry expert over the last 12 months to help us develop our key strategic priorities for the future, and this in itself is a very interesting project. We assumed that we needed to consider big projects and initiatives, but when we looked passionately, what we realised was that there was still a lot of 'low hanging fruit' that needed tackling first. We are therefore focusing on basic housekeeping such as ensuring office space is utilised effectively; re-aligning and releasing space where appropriate and saving costs. We are focused on productivity and time recording throughout the business. We are investing in technology to develop a case management system that will revolutionise the way that we work, saving costs and increasing efficiency.

6.   Bucking the trend for 'big is beautiful', in April 2016 we opened a small local office in Southam which is a vibrant market town about 20 minutes outside of Leamington Spa. There is a lot of house building in the area and a high percentage of

older inhabitants and families, so Conveyancing, Private Client, Wills, and Family work are growing. Local people seem to really appreciate the accessibility of this small friendly local office which is open outside of normal office hours and on Saturday mornings. As mentioned before, we also rather unfashionably remain committed to offering legal advice and support to vulnerable members of our local communities by way of Legal Aid.

What are our future challenges?

There is a lot of discussion always about new means of accessing legal advice. People talk about Tesco Law which hasn't had the expected impact to date at least, and there does seem to remain a view among the general public that they like to see a face and talk to a real person when they are trusting somebody with life changing decisions.

Recruitment and succession planning remain a big challenge and we are always susceptible to changes in the economy. Brexit is of concern because it produces a considerable element of uncertainty and in our particular business, aspects relating to the housing market could impact on areas of our business.

We are also susceptible to changes in government policy. There have been changes to Legal Aid in 2013 which were very significant, and there has been a lot of campaigning within the legal community and some concessions have only just been made, reversing some of the legislation that was restricting the level of Legal Aid being available to victims of domestic abuse. The Government continues to legislate in areas relating to Clinical Negligence and Personal Injury claims. Cybercrime is a huge risk; there are a number of law firms nationally where email hacking and other very clever cybercrimes have caused significant losses. There is also a view that the legal profession, which is so heavily regulated, should be opened up to unqualified people who are not subject to the same regulations as qualified Lawyers, for example, McKenzie Friends who are able to assist Litigants in Person in the Court process and charge for the privilege without having any legal training.

These are all challenges which we at Alsters Kelley choose to see as opportunities!

Erica's top tip:

- You must believe in your business because if you don't, nobody else will. You will have to put your personal, financial and family welfare on the line and if you are not prepared to do that, then ask yourself whether running your own business is really right for you.

- You have to keep going not just for your own benefit but because there are so many other people who are relying on you for their livelihood. This is both a responsibility and a privilege.

- You need to recognise that in every different situation a different set of skills are needed, and you need a team that can provide those. You need staff and colleagues that are good in a crisis, but you also need those that have the skills to develop and implement a strategic vision for the longer term.

- You need to be open to expert assistance and advice; you can't know it all and outsiders (and indeed insiders sometimes, if they are asked) see things that you might have missed. You must be prepared to admit that there are times when you are wrong, and you need help from other sources.

- Finally, you need to know that pizza, red wine, chocolate, cake, and coffee all help!

Erica's favourite quote:

To be successful in business, you need to take to heart the words of Winston Churchill,

"keep buggering on".

You must have a tenacious attitude and you must never give up. I will say that again. You must never give up. Even when it seems you are faced with impossible problems, you just never know what good is around the corner.

www.alsterskelley.com

TWITTER NAME:
@AlstersKelley

Dr Sonya Wallbank
AFBPsS; MCIPD

DIRECTOR
CAPELLAS NURSERIES AND OUT OF SCHOOL CLUBS

"

"DO YOU EVER LOOK AT ANOTHER PERSON AND THINK, 'WOW, SHE REALLY HAS GOT IT ALL', OR, 'WOW, I WISH I COULD DO THAT'? MY MESSAGE IS THAT WE ARE ALL SPECIAL, UNIQUE, PASSIONATE, AND POWERFUL HUMAN BEINGS. HAVING SPENT HOURS WITH PEOPLE WHO ARE AT THEIR LOWEST POINT, YOU RECOGNISE THAT THE SADNESS PEOPLE OFTEN EXPERIENCE COMES FROM NOT RECOGNISING WHAT THEY HAVE, RATHER THAN LOOKING AT WHAT THEY DON'T HAVE.

IF YOU CAN FIND THE EXPERIENCES THAT MAKE YOUR HEART SING, MAKE YOU FEEL HAPPY, AND ENJOY THE GIFT OF TODAY THAN RELISH IN IT; FOR YOU TRULY HAVE IT ALL. IF YOU ARE NOT THERE YET, MAKE CHANGES; LITTLE ONES, HUGE ONES, WHATEVER IT TAKES TO FIND YOUR HAPPY SELF AND NEVER LOOK BACK.

DR SONYA WALLBANK
AFBPsS; MCIPD
CAPELLAS NURSERIES
& OUT OF SCHOOL CLUBS

Having lived approximately half of the average female life expectancy, I have managed to acquire a list of descriptors about myself that I am proud of. Yet, none of them really tell the real story about who I am and what I have the strength to become.

I am blessed to be a mother of three children and have probably paved the way for a lot of mothers behind me to be treated better by their workplaces. I have a Doctorate in Clinical Psychology and specialise in stress and resilience. I am an author of several books and run a consultancy practice, so support individuals and groups to think differently about their own capabilities. I also currently employ 64 people in my nursery and out of school club company, despite leaving school without a single qualification. As 'successful' as my career and work have been, I wrestle with my own self-doubt daily but at least have the tools and training to know how to keep moving forward.

I left home at 15 after a brief but challenging childhood. I was a mixed-up and rebellious teenager who did not respond well to the drink and violence in my home life. I had the benefit of being a clever girl, so from an early age my focus was very much on getting out. I recall being told that I would not survive the night on my own, but I was clearly given the tough gene, as I knew even then, I would never return home.

My first 'proper' job was a Youth Trainee in a Bank. I spent ten years there and worked my socks off every day to achieve my banking qualifications and earn promotion. I was a natural seller and looking back, I loved to listen to people and their stories so never needed to push my sales. Perhaps it was the beginning of my passion about psychology even then. I was highly ambitious and surrounded by a very male culture. I was promoted to Branch Manager at 23 and Regional Manager at 27 but never quite fit the mould. I didn't know enough about football to fit in with my male colleagues and had little interest in lipstick to strike up a meaningful conversation with their wives or girlfriends. Being a successful woman in this environment meant I spent a lot of time isolated and justifying my success, but I was still a Company girl, through and through.

As a top performer in the Bank we enjoyed a typical banker's lifestyle and got to travel around the world on our various sales competitions. I am sure it is a different world now, but this was the nineties and everything was done to excess. I achieved many successful promotions and was the go-to manager for innovation. I never considered doing anything else and really thought I was as valued by my company as much as I valued them.

Life was good, I met my husband to be, but then made the fundamental 'error' of getting pregnant. For the system I worked in, this was a first; a high flyer having a baby, whatever next? I was a grafter and worked until the end of my rather difficult pregnancy. In planning for my return, I was contacted my organisation and told after a measly three months of maternity leave that I was an unknown entity, that to 'prove' myself again I would be given the smallest branch in the country and would need to start again. I was devastated, I spent about five minutes moping before my tough gene kicked in again and I thought, no way was I going to be treated like this after the hard work I had done. I will let you join up the dots, but it did make the headlines.

Having recently come into a sum of money, a newborn baby, and a husband whose company were not exactly enamoured with him, we decided to make a bold move. I began to study psychology with the Open University after being intrigued by the learning that my new baby was exhibiting. We embarked on a journey of travel and work experience that would take us to a range of countries and supporting a range of families with different psychological needs. The opportunity to work with children who were experiencing gun violence and drugs, and help them really did make me and feed my soul to guide me to my next step in the journey.

On becoming pregnant with our second child we returned to the UK. I graduated with a First-Class degree and decided I wanted to train as a Clinical Psychologist. Not having come through the traditional qualification route, I had no idea about how competitive this process was. To train in the UK means that the NHS employs you whilst you learn advanced clinical skills and undertake a Doctorate. What I found out after I had my offer was the myth surrounding training; unless you had traditional qualifications from the right university, knew the right people, and had ticked all the work experience boxes there was no way you would be considered. Of course, I was completely unaware of this and solely focused on what I wanted to do with my life. By this time, I had three children under the age of five and was working for a children's charity part-time.

It was at the time of silly cheap flights to Europe from Birmingham, I applied the first time round thinking I was unlikely to get an interview so had booked a short break to Spain with the family. Having received notification of my interview date which turned out to be right in the middle of my holiday, I knew I would have to fly back even if it was just for the day. I left my husband with the three little ones in Spain and travelled to the airport straight from the beach. I was completely chilled out having spent the morning in the sunshine and realised when I got to the interview perhaps my fellow interviewees were not feeling the same; there was lots of tension and one chap kept leaving the room to be sick. I think even now, my ignorance about the competition saved me, as I was completely oblivious of how much people wanted this.

I was offered a place on the course, they obviously thought that my beach bum chilled attitude would fit. I spent the best three years of my life training and raising our children. We didn't have a lot of money as I was on a training wage and my husband was working part time so we could juggle everything, but we were very happy. There is no feeling more satisfying than helping people who are in mental distress. When you meet someone who is at their lowest, and through their work with you and the work they do for themselves, enable them to participate fully in their life again, or function as a family again, that is a great experience.

Finishing the course, I specialised in child psychology and I knew that I wanted to make a difference. The time I had spent abroad and the experiences of working with people in distress had moved me to want to help and support people to do things differently. The knowledge and skills that I had developed were often in demand when a child or family had reached a very difficult level, and I kept thinking that we could use them earlier and benefit more children. The village that we lived in had a distinct lack of good quality childcare and I knew that if I opened a nursery, I could use all my knowledge to support the staff and children in that work. My banking background made pulling together a business plan easier than it would have been for a novice, and I knew the right people to talk to get the idea financed. The search was on to find a suitable venue, and despite my intensive desire to get the right place, I could not find any property that would work.

Feeling like I may have to put the dream on hold, I started to think about the house we lived in. It would make an ideal nursery as it was on the main road, looked a bit like a Hansel and Gretel house, and would have the right amount of parking. I convinced my husband that moving into rented accommodation and using the house for the nursery was the right thing to do and we embarked on converting the house. I think that single minded thought process is often a driving factor with me; it never crossed my mind that this would not be successful. We were in the right area, with the right qualifications, and we had a strong desire to do things differently.

We opened an after-school club in the May and started straight away to apply some psychological concepts; providing hot-meals freshly cooked for the children after school so that hunger was not driving poor behaviour; having a forum for the children to decide what activities they wanted to do; having a quiet area for homework; and lots of outdoor space for the children to run around.

The nursery conversion was going to require planning permission and here we realised why no other nursery setting had come to the village and stayed. There were lots of groundless objections from older residents and the local committees were very slow to recognise the benefits of extended and quality childcare settings. At one point, I did have to remind myself that it was a nursery we wanted to open and not a contentious nuclear storage site, it really did get silly. One objection was based on a large puddle that may put the children at risk - I did consider arm bands or even a small boat if that would satisfy the concern. One evening, I was reading a story to my little ones when I got the call that the residents association were going to discuss our planning application. I rushed to the meeting armed with my flipcharts and speech prepared- this would be my Erin Brockovich moment for sure. I arrived at the meeting to find one other person in the visitor section who was a tad hard of hearing. I spent the meeting explaining to her what was happening.

Once the residents and their representatives began to be more open minded about the application and could see the quality on offer, they started to offer their support. Eventually, we were granted full planning permission. Even though the planning committee had reservations about a disability scooter meeting our travel train (large buggy with six children) and the carnage that might ensue, they voted predominantly in favour.

The whole experience taught me about the way that our local decisions are made often by people who are largely unaffected by the decisions or issues they are voting on. As one councillor voiced to me – 'do women really have to work all day?' How do we expect our local representatives to be in touch with issues that no longer impact on them? It is our role as women in the community to ensure that we are being represented fairly, and that the decisions which impact on us are not just being made by individuals who are not informed or who are out of date.

We opened our first nursery and were full within three months, a good six months ahead of projections. We now have five sites, 64 members of staff, and celebrate our tenth anniversary this year. We have had a full and challenging ten years with the business but have always kept true to our values that children and families are at the heart of what we do. I have combined the business with a full career maintaining my work within the NHS, University, and at the Department of Health. I had a visit to the Palace recently to meet Prince Charles where I received an award for the stress and resilience work I undertake. I shared the picture with my parents to show how far I had come.

There were many times over the years that I could have taken an easier path, but I want the world to see the difference I make. I want to be a woman who has left a positive mark because of my existence and will do everything I can to make that happen. Last year my husband had a brush with serious ill-health. We have always done everything together and he has been my constant support. Realising that our lives are maybe not forever, it was satisfying to know that I would not have done anything differently. I am still here smiling and practising what I preach. My early years may have challenged me, but they will not define me.

An inspirational story I read a long time ago left me with the message about not just hoping that things would turn out as I wanted, but deciding that they would be that way. Too often in life we complain that things are not as we want them but take no action to change them to be different. So, my one message – don't hope; decide.

Sonya's top tip:

"Believe - have faith in yourself and your
ideas so that you can share this passion
with someone else. No-one will ever feel as
passionately as you do about what you want to do,
so learn how to share this belief with energy and
enthusiasm and people will follow."

Sonya's favourite quote:

"My mission in life is not merely to survive,
but to thrive; and to do so with some passion,
compassion, some humour and some style."

Maya Angelou

www.capellas.co.uk

TWITTER NAME:
@sonyawallbank

Jude Jennison

AUTHOR, SPEAKER, EXECUTIVE COACH
AND HORSE ASSISTED EDUCATOR
LEADERS BY NATURE

"

YOU ARE ONLY LIMITED BY HOW BIG YOU DARE
TO DREAM AND HOW WILLING YOU ARE TO PUT
IN THE WORK TO MAKE IT HAPPEN. SUCCESS CAN
SOMETIMES LOOK EASY BUT LIKE A SWAN, THERE IS
OFTEN A TON OF WORK GOING ON UNDERNEATH.
ASK FOR HELP WHENEVER YOU NEED IT. PEOPLE
ARE OFTEN WILLING TO PROVIDE SUPPORT
WHEN THEY KNOW YOU NEED IT.

JUDE JENNISON
LEADERS BY NATURE

When I was four years old, I declared that I wanted to be either a doctor, a teacher, or a gypsy. I think my current work reflects a combination of all three. My work involves healing people, educating people, and working with horses. At the time, my parents thought I wanted to live in a caravan but it became clear that I was always drawn towards horses.

At the age of nine, I decided I wanted to work outdoors with horses. When I told my parents this, my mum said: 'Don't be ridiculous. It's cold and wet in winter and you can't earn money looking after horses. You need to get yourself a proper job.'

I abandoned the idea and it was 34 years later before horses came back into my life and I fulfilled my dream of working with them.

In a bid to get a 'proper job', I went to university to study French. I graduated in 1990. It was the start of a recession and the first year that all the big companies stopped their graduate training schemes. There were hardly any jobs available and every job I looked at required work experience which I didn't have. In interviews, I was faced with a barrage of discriminating questions and comments such as: 'You'll never get on in an office full of men', 'You can't tell jokes so you won't fit in', and, 'You'll give up and have babies.' I applied for every job in the paper and was rejected from each one. It was a stark introduction to the world of work.

I managed to get a temporary job for three weeks unpacking books and stacking them on shelves at Dillons Bookstore in Coventry, preparing it for opening. Once the shop opened, they offered me a permanent job. I worked there for three years and was promoted three times until I managed the ground floor of the bookshop. I had an annual budget of £1milion. Shops all over Coventry were closing but we continued to meet our targets because we took care to understood our market.

I realised quickly that my forte was the operational side of running a business but if I wanted to develop it in publishing, I needed to be in London. Having recently married, that was not an option but I didn't let limitations constrain me. I knew that I was a manager and a people person and could do that in any sector.

I knew a lot of managers in IBM. One of them said I was the sort of person that IBM should be employing but they were not recruiting graduates. He committed to finding me a job. He recognised that my management skills were of value in a technology company.

One year later, he interviewed me and I joined IBM in 1993. I was the only woman in a sea of 1500 men in the Warwick office. There were a handful of female secretaries and one female manager who left soon after. It was a very different environment from the one I'd been used to in retail. Everybody was technical and everybody was a man. I had no desire to learn anything technical and I persuaded my manager to let me work with customers. They were reluctant at first as everyone else managing clients had technical expertise but eventually they agreed.

I soon won my clients over and gained a reputation for doing a great job cheerfully and quickly. I was moved to pre-sales to help the sales teams negotiate service level agreements and define how the service could be run. My relationship skills and my honest naivety won people over.

In my first management position, I inherited a dysfunctional team of five people, one of whom was about to lose her job. I sat down with them each individually and collectively. I asked them what their aspirations were and helped them achieve them. I was also clear about when their objectives were not achievable. Nobody had been that direct or that supportive before. I resolved the team conflict and turned it around to a high-performing team in six months. For the first time the team were being listened to, not just for technical expertise, but as human beings. I had no support in doing this so I followed my instincts, wanting to do the right thing for everyone.

Having turned a low-performing team round to a high-performing team, my management career began in earnest. I did a variety of leadership roles, leading UK, European, and global teams. I had 17 roles in 16 years and as many managers. I became known for challenging the status quo. I was often given roles that were undefined, unclear, and needed structure and governance putting into place.

In one particular role, I was the Business Operations Leader across Europe. I was responsible for the non-people cost of running the outsourcing business, including the data centres, and the hardware and software in it. There was no team in place so I visited the major countries in Europe and persuaded the General Managers to give me someone to join my team.

I had no authority over the team but I had a huge responsibility to reduce the $1 billion budget by 10%. I reduced it by $126 million in year one and a further $132 million in year two. I put in place solid management systems and governance and provided a foundation for future strategic and operational work to be delivered at a European level.

Every role I did required me to influence others without authority – either managing clients, European or global teams, or project teams of diverse and disparate people. Nearly all my roles required me to build relationships virtually so I had the added challenge of sensing on the phone who was paying attention and who wasn't. I worked hard to build relationships and keep everyone engaged. I was known for being driven because I had made it clear I was ambitious, but I delivered by winning people over. I didn't always realise that until later because my managers always focused on the results, but the way I achieved those results was always relational.

In July 2000, I started to learn to ride. After six lessons, I fell off a horse, broke nine ribs, my shoulder blade in each corner, and had a collapsed lung. I ended up in intensive care, narrowly missed a cardiac arrest, and was an inch away from being a paraplegic. it was six months before I returned to work part-time.

I initially returned to work for two hours a day. My back spasmed so much I would regularly drive home in tears. I was given back office functions that were not much more than admin. I was bored and frustrated and it was a challenging two years before I could work full-time again. I had two further near-death experiences around horses, resulting in me being terrified of them.

In 2008, I went to a women's international conference in Rome. I was inspired by women doing amazing work in the world and I knew I was ready to broaden my horizons. I set upon training as a coach, starting with IBM's Coaching as a Manager course, followed by an 18-month coaching training program external to IBM. I continued to do a variety of different senior leadership roles and coached people alongside my day job.

In 2009, I'd been travelling extensively visiting a different country in Europe nearly every week and I was close to burnout. I took a year sabbatical so I could reflect on where my career was going next. When I took a break, my body went into shut down for about six weeks. I was so exhausted that when I did finally stop I couldn't get going again. I could barely move.

I reframed the year to get myself fit and well. In parallel I attended a year-long leadership programme which gave me the courage to leave IBM in July 2010. I left knowing that I had loved almost every moment of every job and had done great work. I was moving towards something new rather than away from something I didn't like. It was a courageous thing to do to leave a well-loved career and step into the unknown.

When I left, I set up a leadership and coaching business. The first contract I delivered was a six-month programme called Challenge the Status Quo. At the time, it was out there. Under my leadership, I watched a group of 12 ground-down, exhausted male directors come alive. I saw them open their hearts, learn to trust, and connect human being to human being. It was life-changing for them and life-changing for me. When one of them said: 'I've found my inner peace', I knew I was having the impact I wanted to have.

In March 2011, I challenged this group of directors to overcome their fear of something so that they could explore what happens when we are scared, how we can overcome fear, and what that means for our leadership. I'm a great believer in walking my talk so I decided to overcome my fear of horses. I googled coaching and horses and found someone to help me. In five minutes, I overcame my fear, and in two hours I learned so much about my leadership that when he announced that he was running a train the trainer session three weeks later, I found myself booked on to it.

I had no intention of running Leadership with Horses workshops because I knew nothing about horses but throughout that week, I realised that what I lacked in horsemanship skills, I had in leadership skills; I could get the horses to do anything I wanted because I was clear, open, honest and built a relationship with them. I invited them to work with me, not for me. I realised this was what I had been doing in IBM all along. By contrast, some of the people with lots of horse experience were struggling; they didn't have the leadership skills and experience I had. In July 2011, I became the first person to qualify as a Horse Assisted Educator without any prior horse experience.

In September 2011, my coach challenged me to get clients to work with the horses. I sent an email to 100 people offering a two for one workshop if they paid for it by the end of the month. Ten people signed up and paid so I thought, I'd better get a horse!

My first horse was called Kalle. She was 12 years old and a powerful mare. She was highly spirited, intuitive, and sensitive. She was not ideal for a novice like me in those early days but deep down I knew she was right for me. She connected on such a deep level.

I had daily dramas looking after a horse that I knew nothing about. I was bullied by the yard staff who thought I should slap my horse when she was naughty. She reared up after electrocuting us both on the electric fence and re-triggered my original trauma. After being face down in mud with concussion, everyone told me to give up and get a proper job. Instead, I took on a second horse, expanding my one-to-one coaching with horses to include workshops for teams.

I overcame so many challenges that I wrote my first book, Leadership beyond measure, which I self-published in May 2015. At the same time, I launched a new business called The Leadership Whisperers with a business partner. We continued to push the boundaries of what was possible, winning Woman Who... Start-up Award in our first year and Finalist for Woman Who... Export Award in our second year of operation.

The Leadership Whisperers never made a profit and we ceased trading on 30th June 2017. The five horses immediately became my personal responsibility and cost. I had a choice – to get a well-paid corporate job or set up again and make it work. My business partner kept the brand name, and I was left with the liability of five horses and associated costs. I gave myself three months on my own, not long considering I was a start-up with the costs of an established business.

I borrowed money to pay the cost of the horses for the first month. In the first weekend on my own, I launched my new business Leaders by Nature and created my own website with no budget. In the first two months, I signed enough work to cover my costs for the first six months. This was twice the amount of work I had signed in the previous six months with my business partner. I was focused, committed, and determined to keep the horses and continue the life-changing work that I was doing.

Since re-launching as Leaders by Nature in July 2017, I've made a profit, gained repeat business from clients, and delivered workshops to new clients in Germany, Poland, and Hungary. I've written my second book, Leading Through Uncertainty, obtained a publishing contract with a traditional publisher and launched a Leading Through Uncertainty podcast, where I interview CEOs and senior leaders from large corporations, as well as local dignitaries who have great stories to tell.

In February 2018, I became a finalist for the FSB West Midlands Triumph Over Adversity award, in recognition of the repeated challenges I've faced and overcome throughout my career, and in March 2018, I became a Finalist for Woman Who... Achieves Solopreneur Award.

In December 2017, I became a Trustee on the Board for Heart of England Community Foundation; a recognition of my leadership experience and desire to give back to the local community. Throughout the course of my career, I've been focused on what I can do to make the world a better place - while I worked at IBM, I had two black Labradors who were breeding stock for Guide Dogs for the Blind. I was midwife to seven litters of puppies over seven years; a total of 60 puppies who have gone on to be trained as Guide Dogs.

In the last five years, I've mentored (for free) eight people from all over the world (Dubai, China, Switzerland, USA, as well as UK) through a year-long leadership programme and am highly regarded amongst that community; my name has become well known for providing great mentoring, meaning I often get asked to mentor a lot of people.

I've provided free advice to Leadership with Horses practitioners in Germany, Russia, Poland, and the US, and helped them develop their offerings and marketing to get their businesses off the ground. I have been asked to present at every global Leadership with Horses conference since I started this work in 2012.

Since re-launching as Leaders by Nature, I have expanded my services as a Strategic Leadership Partner to help executive and senior leadership teams align around their strategy and key objectives. I help them create behavioural change in their organisation through my podcast and books, as an inspirational speaker, facilitator and Leadership with Horses.

I continuously develop myself and push the boundaries of what is possible, drawing on my extensive business experience and ability to challenge the status quo with courage and compassion. I believe that conscious leadership matters and makes a huge difference in our homes, the workplace and society.

Jude's top tip:

"Find the skill, commitment, and your
tribe of supporters so that you can achieve
whatever you want to achieve. Whenever you
are struggling, one of the three is missing.

If you don't have all the skills needed
to meet your goal, learn them.

If you lack commitment, decide if the goal
is important enough, then either commit
or change direction.

Build a support network who can support you
practically and emotionally to stay on track. "

Jude's favourite quote:

"If you can lead a horse, you can lead anyone."

Jude Jennison

www.judejennison.com

TWITTER NAME:
@judejennison

FIND OUT MORE ABOUT
Woman Who...

The Woman Who...Achieves Awards celebrate the achievements of women in business and Rising Stars of the future, who are currently in education or training. Quite simply our aim is to:

Inspire...Achieve...Celebrate

The Awards take place in the Midlands each year. Further Awards events will take place in other regions during 2019.

The Woman Who...Achieves Network was set up to ensure that we retain momentum in between each annual Awards and highlights the issues that women in business face on a day to day basis. Sandra Garlick sits on the FSB's Women in Enterprise Taskforce and feeds back issues from the various Network meetings.

The Network meets quarterly at venues throughout the UK and offers the chance to network and listen to local inspiring speakers sharing their business story, their challenges and how they overcame them. Men are also welcome to attend.

If you are interested in organising a Woman Who...Achieves Network in your area, please contact us with your details.

Email: contact@womanwho.co.uk

Web: www.womanwho.co.uk

THE

Woman Who... Judges

LEFT TO RIGHT

*Ian O'Donnell, MBE, Dr Sharon Redrobe, OBE,
Emma Heathcote-James, Paul Carvell*

I AM A WOMAN WHO...

2018

Sponsors & Partners

Thank you for your support

With Special Thanks

*"Coombe Abbey Hotel are delighted to support the Woman Who...
Achieves Awards for the 3rd year running and to be chosen for
the photoshoot for the cover of this book. We look forward to
supporting future inspirational events celebrating and recognising
the achievements of Women in Business."*

June Picken, Director of Sales, Coombe Abbey Hotel

www.coombeabbey.com

*"Imaginate have thoroughly enjoyed supporting the design and
photography for 'I Am A Woman Who'. From an initial idea by our
Studio Manager, Sarah Young, to managing the photoshoot with
International Photographer, Simon Derviller, creating the design
of the book itself and being asked to feature as a contributor, it has
been an inspirational and exciting project to be part of. We look
forward to working with Woman Who... on future projects."*

Joanne Derviller, MD, Imaginate Creative

www.imaginate.uk.com